D-DAY
TO BERLIN

THE LONG MARCH TO
VICTORY

First published in 2013

A catalogue record for this book is available from the British Library

ISBN: 978-0-85733-210-3

Published by Haynes Publishing, Sparkford, Yeovil,
Somerset BA22 7JJ, UK
Tel: 01963 442030 Fax: 01963 440001
Int. tel: +44 1963 442030 Int. fax: +44 1963 440001
E-mail: sales@haynes.co.uk
Website: www.haynes.co.uk

Haynes North America Inc., 861 Lawrence Drive,
Newbury Park, California 91320, USA

Images © Mirrorpix

Creative Director: Kevin Gardner
Designed for Haynes by BrainWave

Printed and bound in the US

D-DAY TO BERLIN

THE LONG MARCH TO VICTORY

David Edwards

Introduction

D-Day noun

1. The day, 6 June 1944, on which the Allied invasion of Europe began.

2. The day on which any large-scale operation is planned to start.

◀ British troops pour on to a Normandy beach under fire from German pill-boxes.

So far the Commanders who are engaged report that everything is proceeding according to plan. And what a plan! This vast operation is undoubtedly the most complicated and difficult that has ever taken place … The battle that has now begun will grow constantly in scale and in intensity for many weeks to come, and I shall not attempt to speculate upon its course.

— **Winston Churchill, House of Commons, 6 June 1944, D-Day**

What a plan, indeed. Many, at home and abroad, had been demanding a plan such as D-Day for two years or more, but once details of the massed Allied landings in Normandy on 6 June 1944 began to be known, and as the battle for Normandy, for France, for Europe unravelled over the following months, it became clear why it had taken so long to come together.

Nearly 200,000 Allied servicemen were put ashore on five Normandy beaches, codenamed Sword, Juno, Gold, Omaha and Utah. The Allies sent 1,200 fighting ships into action, more than 5,000 vessels in all, and 10,000 aircraft lent powerful support.

Mobilising an operation of that scale took time. Planning for its success was a lengthy business too. And arguments and disagreements between the Allies merely added to the sense of impatience and frustration that had grown since early 1942.

Stalin's Russian Army was fighting a bloody and costly war against the Germans on the Eastern Front – the First Front – and the Russian dictator was desperate for Britain and her allies to come to his aid in 1942. Stalin implored Churchill and the American President, Franklin D. Roosevelt, to launch an offensive against Hitler in Western Europe, to take the pressure and some of Germany's military might off the Russians.

Increasingly, also, the Americans in the shape of Roosevelt and General Eisenhower were keen to act. Churchill, meanwhile, played the middle ground, preferring aerial attacks and manoeuvres in North Africa and subsequently Italy to the danger of a full-on landing in France.

Fresh in his mind were the events of August 1942. A top-secret raid on the French port of Dieppe, heavily fortified by the occupying German forces, was hoped to be stage one of a co-ordinated attack on mainland Europe. It went disastrously wrong and all thoughts of direct military action across the Channel were put firmly on the back burner. If troops were to be put ashore safely and in sufficient numbers then the plans needed ripping up and to be started again.

Over the next 21 months, that preparation took place. The pages of the *Daily Mirror* did not always reflect what was going on, as much of it was behind closed doors and strictly confidential. But those pages do reflect the mood of the time: the fear, the impatience, the stoicism, the heroism of servicemen and of civilians too. And through them we discover how millions of British citizens learnt of the momentous events going on around them.

And once the D-Day operation itself was launched, and as the crucial days and weeks after 6 June 1944 unfolded, we see how history was written and captured on camera as it happened.

So much of what we know about the Second World War comes from history books, school history lessons, films, TV documentaries: all written with the benefit of hindsight and the knowledge of how it ended. The following pages do not have that. Instead they have raw, fresh reports, ones pieced together in newspaper offices from censored wartime sources, from reporters embedded with Allied troops and from the streets of Britain, telling the story as best they could. They are accompanied by many photographs and cartoons used by the *Daily Mirror*, conveying some of the horrors but also the reality of a brutal war.

All in all it makes for a remarkably informative and fresh perspective on one of the most compelling chapters in human history.

Wednesday, June 7, 1944   THE DAILY MIRROR   Page 3

DESTINY'S HOUR

THE hour of destiny for Europe, and perhaps for the whole of mankind, has struck. A simple announcement, followed by the homely tones of General Eisenhower on the radio, proclaimed a world-shaking event, the like of which has no parallel in history. What began in Northern France yesterday morning marks the final phase in the greatest war of all time, and is the largest, most elaborate, most intrepid operation of its kind ever undertaken. Our first thoughts in this solemn hour must be with the men of the Allied Armies who have landed with our banners—the banners of Hope and Freedom—and are determined, despite all dangers and difficulties, to carry them across Europe and in due course to plant them in the heart of Berlin. Some of these men have fought in many lands and have won much glory. Others are newer to the bloody game of war, but are of great heart. The task before them may be stupendous, but they will perform it stupendously. It is impossible to say how long this final phase of the struggle will last. Possibly it will reach its inevitable end quicker than some people suppose. While there is, at present, every sign that the enemy will fight with skill and desperate energy, there remains the one great imponderable factor of how the German people react to a war which is inexorably drawing closer and closer to German soil. Meantime there are hard days to endure.

★

On a memorable occasion, and at a time when there seemed little left to us except hope and that sublime obstinacy which is the British character expressed in terms of adversity, the Prime Minister, with inspiring pessimism, promised us blood, tears, and sweat. It is blood, tears and sweat that we face again today, but in a very different mood. Then the skies were grey. Now they are ablaze with the light of triumphs achieved, and victory to come. On behalf of those who have gone forth in courage and cheerful fortitude to fight this epic battle we, at home, offer our prayers, and pledge ourselves to support them in mind, in spirit, in material, to the utmost of our capacity. The curtain rises on the closing scene of the greatest human conflict the world has ever known. To many people this is a holy war because it represents the eternal struggle between Good and Evil. As our hearts swell with pride and awe; as we contemplate the perils and glories of the battle; as we offer up our humble supplication; we can, with reason, select a sacred invocation for the battle cry, and say, with Montgomery: "Let God arise, and let His enemies be scattered." **B. B. B.**

The hour of reckoning

7

Calls for a Second Front

January – August **1942**

With Stalin's Red Army fighting Germany on the Eastern Front in Russia, there was a growing clamour in the West to establish a second front on mainland Europe. Stalin himself was desperate for help from Britain and America. President Roosevelt, following the Japanese attack on Pearl Harbour in December 1941, was similarly enthusiastic to engage German forces in Europe. Against this tide, Winston Churchill urged caution, preferring to win the naval battle in the Atlantic, confront the Axis powers in North Africa and the Far East and bomb Germany to gradually sap its strength. All of this took time; but by early 1942 there were impatient critics at home as well as among the Allies . . .

Winston Churchill, Britain's Prime Minister, and President Roosevelt of America meet on board the USS *Augusta* off the coast of Newfoundland in August 1941, the first of many meetings during the Second World War.

DAILY MIRROR, Friday, June 12, 1942.

Daily Mirror

JUNE 12

No. 12,011   ONE PENNY
Registered at the G.P.O. as a Newspaper.

20-year pact with Russia means

M. Molotov

A SECOND FRONT IN 1942

Post-war arms aid | Planning peace

BY OUR POLITICAL CORRESPONDENT

BRITAIN and Russia have signed a "peace and war" Treaty of mutual assistance to last for twenty years.

A crowded House of Commons cheered again and again when Mr. Anthony Eden made this announcement last night. M. Molotov, Russia's Foreign Minister, Mr. Eden revealed, has been in London, in Washington, and back again in London without a word of his journeyings reaching the public in either country.

But more than the signing of one of the most important treaties in world history was accomplished.

Full understanding was reached between the leaders of both countries with regard to the "urgent task of creating a second front in Europe in 1942."

Mr. Eden seemed to stress the date in his speech—and the House reared its approval.

In Washington, M. Molotov discussed the same matter with President Roosevelt and arrived at a complete agreement with him.

Staff Chiefs at Talks

In London the British Chiefs of Staff took part in the discussions regarding a second front this year, most of the conversations being carried on at Chequers, the Prime Minister's country house.

The complete harmony in which agreement was reached on all points is shown by the fact that M. Molotov reached here on May 20, after a hazardous journey, delayed considerably by bad weather, and had left for Washington exactly seven days later.

The Treaty had been signed the day before, and he flew the Atlantic with the text of it in his pocket to show to President Roosevelt.

There were further talks on his return to London, when he bore with him the American Government's approval of all that had been decided.

Now he is back in Moscow to report to M. Stalin on the outstanding success of his mission.

I understand that although they are not mentioned in the Treaty, the thorny problem of the western frontiers was discussed at length and appreciable progress, towards which the Poles played a part, was made in laying the foundation for a future settlement.

The Pact—given in full on

Garrison quit Bir Hakeim

BIR Hakeim, Libya fortress, has fallen. The Free French garrison which had defied furious Axis onslaughts for sixteen days was withdrawn by order of General Ritchie on Wednesday night.

The withdrawal was announced last night after the German and Italian High Command had claimed the capture of the fortress. Berlin said it was taken by storm in the late morning hours of yesterday.

The Germans paid a tribute to the gallantry of the fighting French garrison in stressing the "bitter resistance offered for many days."

Drive East Now?

The last surrender demand was made by a German officer. General Koenig, the French commander, watched as he set off on the return journey with the usual reply.

Suddenly the Nazi car missed its course, swerved into a minefield and was blown up.

After that the Germans were satisfied with waving white flags at the defenders.

Rommel may now be able to go ahead with an all-out drive eastwards.

Berlin radio says that while dive-bombers attacked Bir Hakeim incessantly, bombers and fighters prevented the Allies from bringing up reinforcements.

A gap was made in the minefields, but troops and tanks came up against another strong defensive system. Dive-bombers and artillery battered the inner defences.

"It's murder," said a radio reporter, amid the sound of heavy gunfire. "They are encircled from the north, south, east and west. Every hour supplies try to get through, but are blown up or left in flames."

THEY DIDN'T KNOW IT WAS MOLOTOV

M. Molotov arrived by special train at a tiny English station. No one knew he was coming. No one recognised him when he came. This is the story of the village that missed its Big Day.

By E. H. CHRISTIAN ("Daily Mirror" Reporter)

A TINY country station in the damp coolness of the evening . . . a train drew in and stopped . . . a world-famous diplomat alighted.

There were no cheering crowds. There were no ceremonial presentations.

That is how M. Molotov, Russian Foreign Minister, arrived.

I was the only journalist present to see this great occasion. It was a world scoop which I could not use.

M. Molotov arrived from the north in a seven-coach special train. He came to a station on the outskirts of London, set in fields, with a few houses in the nearby village.

George, the station master, and his one porter were the staff to greet this "special."

A contingent of Air Force men and police arrived well before the train was due.

They had not long to wait, for the train was ahead of schedule.

A number of large cars arrived later, bearing Mr. Eden, M. Maisky, and other members of the welcoming party.

Even Anthony Eden's well-known face attracted no crowd. The only members of the public present, apart from the Daily Mirror photographer and myself, were two village women.

They were so concerned with catching their train that they had no thought for the identity or importance of the visitor.

No Ceremony

The meeting of M. Molotov and the welcoming party was without ceremony.

The Foreign Commissar, hatless, and dressed in a grey suit, stepped from the train and shook hands with Mr. Eden, M. Maisky, and other officials, smiling broadly. Mr. Eden also seemed in excellent spirits.

The greetings on the platform were brief. A faint drizzle sprayed the party as it straggled up the incline from the station to the road. Mr. Eden

led the way, with M. Molotov and M. Maisky following side by side.

While waiting for the cars to be brought up, M. Molotov stood, hatless, talking to his Ambassador and Mr. Eden.

The informality was out of keeping with the importance of the occasion.

Day of Rumours

Filled with officials, the first car moved forward. M. Molotov and M. Maisky entered the second car with two of their staff. They shook hands again as they parted from Mr. Eden.

"Till tomorrow, then," said our Foreign Secretary, as he smiled goodbye.

Within half an hour the occasion was over. The village had missed its big moment. George was once again issuing tickets.

Next morning the village buzzed with rumours about the visitor. They ranged from Stalin to Roosevelt.

But until the villagers read this story they will not know for certain his identity.

Second front thrills U.S.

Announcement of the plans for a second front in 1942 has thrilled America, says Reuter from Washington.

The implication is that shipping difficulties will not be allowed to stand in the way.

It is also assumed that the forthcoming big air raids by British and American forces will constitute the preliminary action.

News of the Anglo-Soviet Treaty was given to Russia in an announcement broadcast by all Soviet radio stations, whose programmes were interrupted.

Molotov's Washington Talks.—Back page.

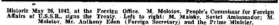

Historic May 26, 1942, at the Foreign Office. M. Molotov, People's Commissar for Foreign Affairs of U.S.S.R., signs the Treaty. Left to right: M. Maisky, Soviet Ambassador; M. Molotov, Mr. Anthony Eden (Foreign Secretary) and the Prime Minister.

Continued on Back Page

Mastery can only be regained by furious, unrelenting assault.—The Prime Minister.

Winston Churchill and the French Prime Minister Paul Reynaud urge the Allied boxer to change tactics and go on the attack in May 1940.

7 January 1942

YANKS ARE COMING OVER HERE: F.D.R.'S BIG PLAN

AMERICA is to send armed forces to Britain. She will build up an overwhelming superiority of munitions and ships over the Axis nations. She will arm the conquered peoples of the world to revolt against their oppressors.

President Roosevelt made these declarations in his message to Congress last night.

"American land, air and sea forces," he said, "will take stations in the British Isles, which constitute an essential fortress in this world struggle.

"The American armed forces must be used at any place in all the world where it seems advisable to engage the forces of the enemy.

"In some cases these operations will be defensive in order to protect key positions.

"In other cases these operations will be offensive in order to strike at the common enemy with a view to his complete encirclement and eventual total defeat.

"American armed forces will operate at many points in the Far East. American armed forces will on all the oceans be helping to guard essential communications which are vital to the United Nations.

"American armed forces will help protect this hemisphere and also bases outside this hemisphere which could be used for an attack on the Americas."

VAST PRODUCTION PLAN

Mr. Roosevelt announced an overwhelming production plan – "so overwhelming that the Axis nations can never hope to catch up with it."

"The United States must build planes, tanks, guns and ships to the utmost capacity to produce arms not only for our own forces, but also for the armies, navies and air forces fighting on our side.

"And our overwhelming superiority must be adequate to put weapons at the proper time into the hands of those men in the conquered nations who stand ready to seize the first opportunity to revolt.

"Our task is hard, our task is unprecedented, and time is short.

"In a word, it means an all out war by individual effort and family effort in a united country.

"Only this all-out scale of production will hasten the ultimate all-out victory.

"Speed will count. Lost ground can always be regained, lost time never."

Referring to U.S. losses in the Pacific, the President said: "We have already tasted defeat. We may suffer further setbacks.

"We must face the fact of a hard, long, bloody and costly war.

"The world is too small to provide adequate living room for both Hitler and God."

15 January 1942

NEAR AND FAR

WHEN the Prime Minister chooses to return to his own country he will find a very different atmosphere from that in which he left for America.

We may suppose that Mr. Churchill's mind is full of the long-term plans which he has so successfully arranged with Mr. Roosevelt. But we fear that it will be useless to describe them, in well-chosen phrases, to the House of Commons.

For Parliamentary and public indignation over the bungling incompetence, and complacency that have placed Singapore and Australia in dire peril cannot be quieted by cheerio promises to the effect that in 1945 the Grand Alliance will possess a million aeroplanes, that twenty million tanks will be rolling along in 1950, and that, before the end of the century, when all the Blimps now muddling the war are, thank God, dead, our superiority over the enemy will be so immense that we shall at last be able to take the initiative on a large scale. The public here, and, for good reasons, in Australia, are sick of far-off visions, sick of the distance that lends no enchantment to the nearer view.

We want swift and sure decisions for the present, not rosy prophecies about the future. We want speed in immediate action, not lumbering preparations that may never be completed if we lose battle after battle and never reach the great battle that we have to

Russian Ballet!

This is dangerous rubbish. Peoples are responsible for the governments they tolerate and encourage. When the Fascists treacherously entered the war the "gentle" Italian people, as a whole, were excited and pleased. Their dark eyes glistened at the prospect of gain. In the years before did cruelty and aggression in Africa even once evoke the voice of protest? No, not even from the Holy See.

◀ The German Army had become locked in a stalemate in the autumn of 1941 when faced with determined Soviet opposition at Leningrad and Sevastopol. Russian resistance was fuelling calls at home for Allied action.

21 January **1942**

MOJAISK FALLS: BIGGEST VICTORY FOR RUSSIANS

MOJAISK, Hitler's last stronghold on the road to Moscow – a blazing hell in which the cream of the Nazi troops had been ordered to fight to the death – was yesterday recaptured by the Russians.

The announcement was made in a special Soviet communiqué last night.

The town, the communiqué said, fell after fierce hand-to-hand fighting in the streets and blazing buildings. Some prisoners were taken.

About 100,000 of Hitler's picked troops had been holding on grimly to Mojaisk while the Soviet armies pressed relentlessly forward north and south of the town.

FLEEING NAZIS

Last night Stalin's Army was celebrating what it considered to be its greatest victory of the war. The achievement crowned nearly eight weeks of an offensive in the bitter Russian winter after a Soviet

win. While we crawl to the remote goal we might easily fall into a pit.

Will Mr. Churchill act and act swiftly? Will he see the red light bang in front of him, and cease gazing at the dim meteors glimmering far, far away?

19 January **1942**

THE GENTLE WOP!

FOOLISHNESS dies hard. Having tired for the time being of telling us about the "nice German", the one-time appeasers have begun to enlist our sympathies on behalf of the gentle Wop! In other words, a large section of the Italian people are said to have no more in common with Mussolini and his gang than the "good" Germans have with the Nazi tyrants!

retreat almost to the gates of Moscow.

Mojaisk, which lies sixty miles west of Moscow, was captured by the Germans on October 14. Remnants of the German forces defeated by the Russians at Kondrovo – a town in the Smolensk region which Monday night's Soviet communiqué also reported had been recaptured – are fleeing in disorder, pursued by the Russians, according to Moscow.

27 January 1942

◀ The first American troops arrive in Northern Ireland.

YANKS ARE OVER: U.S. INFANTRY IN N IRELAND

GERMAN raiders were over Northern Ireland in daylight yesterday, a few hours after several thousand American infantry, fully equipped and with field artillery, had landed there.

Air defences were in action, but there were no bombs.

Mr. Henry L. Stimson, U.S. War Secretary, announced the arrival in Washington last night, twenty days after President Roosevelt promised in his speech to Congress that "American land, air and sea forces will take stations in the British Isles, which constitutes an essential fortress in this world struggle."

The Americans will take up barracks at bases prepared for them in Northern Ireland. Technicians from their country built camps of Nissen huts for them – cities where American food and cigarettes and entertainment will make them feel at home.

Sir Archibald Sinclair, the Air Minister who welcomed the Americans, told them: "Your safe arrival here marks a new stage in the world war.

The Mayflower returns. *President Roosevelt asked for £14,000,000 to fight the Axis, and the beginnings of the mighty flood of American troops reached Britain.*
(February 28, 1942)

"It is no isolated manoeuvre of war but part of the general disposition of our forces which is being made under the supreme responsibility of your President and our Prime Minister.

"It is a gloomy portent for Mr. Hitler, nor will its significance be lost on General Tojo.

"The Philippines, the Dutch East Indies and British territory in the Far East are being ravaged.

"All this is in the minds of responsible leaders who are planning our joint strategy and your welcome arrival here today reveals part of one great plan to smash the dictator Powers wherever they may be found."

Locals greet the arrival of a US Navy destroyer in a Northern Ireland port, January 1942.

28 January 1942

HE ASKS WHY

Demanding to know why an American Expeditionary Force had been sent to the British Isles instead of to the Philippines, Mr. John Robsion, in the U.S. House of Representatives, said yesterday Britain had three and a half million men "armed to the teeth and sitting on their bottoms."

9 February 1942

IT'S UP TO US TO SMASH HITLER IN SPRING

CAN YOU DO MORE TO HELP?

By SIR STAFFORD CRIPPS, who spoke in Bristol yesterday afternoon, and gave the Postscript on the radio last night

IT is up to us all – to you and to me – to see that we play our full part in defeating the coming offensive . . . any idea that the maximum effort is no longer necessary or that we can leave the Russians to defeat Germany alone is absolutely false.

There now stands between Hitler, and a certain and not too long delayed defeat, the chance that he may be strong enough to renew his offensive with success in the spring.

In the month of April it may become possible for him to launch a fresh attack in the south of Russia towards the much-coveted and much-needed oil of the Caucasus.

He will probably concentrate all his force in that direction – a new and terrific blitz planned with the meticulous care of the German mind.

Therefore, an even greater effort to win the war must be made in this country. Had our efforts in production been greater, we should not now be retreating in North Africa.

If we work with 100 per cent effort, sacrifice our private interests, and give to Russia all the support we can, then, in my view, there is every chance of Germany being defeated by this time next year.

We must not make recent Russian successes an excuse for a relaxation of our efforts.

When I complimented Mr. Kalinin, President of the U.S.S.R., on the Russian advances, he stressed to me the dangers of over-confidence.

RUSSIA NEEDS MORE AID

The moral of the fighting that is now proceeding is not that we can send less help to Russia, but that we must send more. The Russian losses are heavy and the expenditure of ammunition, planes and tanks is very large indeed.

While at the moment we may not be able to help with men, we can and must help with arms of every kind, with raw materials and with foodstuffs.

I do not believe that the country, taken as a whole, has any reservations whatever as to their desire for full friendship and co-operation with the U.S.S.R., but there are still those who look at the question from the point of view of the old fear complex.

PARTNERSHIP

Such people must not be allowed to influence our relations with Russia in a negative direction. Either we have a partnership with Russia in the reconstruction of Europe or we plunge the world again into chaos.

Hoarders, of food, black marketeers and others are given short shrift in Russia. It would be difficult for the Russians to understand the tolerance we show to them here.

The turning eastwards of the Nazi hordes has for the time at least relieved this country from the threat of invasion.

We must now make it certain that no such attempt will ever be made against our shores, that our daughters and wives will never have to suffer the ghastly horrors that have befallen the Russian women.

YOUR EFFORT

Can you do more than you are doing now to help the common cause?

Your individual effort is your personal responsibility. You cannot get out of it by the criticism of others.

I am not asking you to criticise your neighbour, but to examine your own effort.

To have regard to personal interests, or to allow the post-war interests of your company or your business to influence your present actions is to fail your country, in this most critical moment. We are out to win this war; there must be no reservations.

I have felt in this country since my return a lack of urgency.

Today our needs and those of our Russian allies are as great and as pressing.

Victory still hangs in the balance so long as men and women hesitate to play their full part.

◗ Sir Stafford Cripps addresses an Anglo-Soviet Youth Friendship Alliance meeting in Westminster, March 1942.

9 February **1942**

THE TIME IS NOW

A POUND of action is worth a ton of words. If victory could have been achieved by speeches, blue-prints, production estimates, rosy raptures and every variety of burbling optimism, the war would have been over almost before it began.

Our great Ally across the Atlantic seems to be going through a phase strangely similar to a part of our own recent and rather melancholy history. She is doing tremendous things, on paper and from the platform. Her production schedules are gigantic. Her armed forces will as year succeeds year, become colossal. Hitler and Tojo, one would think, must be shivering in their shoes.

Hitler and Tojo are doing nothing of the kind. They are just hurrying, hurrying, hurrying. They know that what is done today is more important than what may be done tomorrow.

Of course it is necessary to look ahead. Forward planning is the hard foundation of strategy. Lack of foresight in the past has led to grievous occurrences, and it is good to find that the Americans are determined to prepare for what may happen years hence. But may we suggest that what is happening *now* is even more important. Hitler and Tojo won't politely *wait* to be beaten. They will go all out to win themselves *now*.

The great offensive they are preparing for this spring cannot be met with machines swarming off the production lines in 1945. So let everyone, on both sides of the Atlantic, get rid at once of that future complex.

The time to do things is now. Mr. Nelson, production dictator in the United States, is, we are thankful to say, working on that principle. Flowery estimates and futurist prophecies do not interest him. He wants the goods delivered at once.

Does American industry appreciate this Nelson touch? Have we in this country completely got rid of the habit of thinking that to talk is as good as to act? Do we realise that the guiding principles of our war effort must be that (1) today is better than tomorrow; (2) he makes twice who makes quickly?

Our new Minister of Production will doubtless impress these truths upon the whole industrial organisation of Great Britain. Moreover, Lord Beaverbrook, we are convinced, is capable of the most realistic co-operation with his colleague overseas. If he is fond of slogans he might suggest, "Work now and talk another time."

LITVINOV TELLS US TO RISK IT, ATTACK NOW

NOW is the time for a second front. Inaction will lose the war. Attack may win it.

This was the keynote of a speech made by Comrade Litvinov, Soviet Ambassador to the U.S., in New York last night.

If Hitler's strained armies on the Eastern Front can be weakened by a diversion elsewhere, it will be possible for the Soviet forces to drive the Huns back further – "to Berlin and beyond."

"The more we console ourselves with general statements about the impossibility of losing the war the further we shall be from looking for realistic ways to victory," said M. Litvinov.

"There may be a much greater actual risk in waiting and doing nothing, in letting slip one opportunity after another.

"Action involving risk has at any rate some chance of success, whereas inaction also involving risk is practically never crowned with success."

"WORTH SOME RISK"
M. Litvinov said that although the war might drag on through

Daily Mirror — Front Page

DAILY MIRROR, Tuesday, March 17, 1942.

Daily Mirror

No. 11,937 . ONE PENNY
Registered at the G.P.O. as a Newspaper.

Map shows the invasion danger points of Australia. The Japanese forces are in New Guinea in some strength, and also on Timor Island. A Port Moresby (Papua) message says it is believed that the Japs are attempting to probe cautiously, establishing bases in New Guinea for an attack on the fertile eastern coast of Australia, by-passing Darwin, behind which is waterless desert.

NEW JAP AUSTRALIA MOVE

DARWIN, vital port of North Australia, was again raided by Japanese bombers yesterday, in preparation for a large-scale invasion of the Commonwealth the Japanese are reported to be withdrawing troops from China. They are being embarked, some for Burma and some for Australia.

Fourteen bombers swooped over Darwin in two waves. There were casualties, announced Mr. Curtin, Australian Prime Minister. The Japs mostly dropped an anti-personnel type of bomb. Damage was slight.

Paris radio, quoting Tokio, claims that the port of Darwin has been "completely destroyed."

Although heavily outnumbered, nine U.S. Army fighters destroyed three Japanese planes in a combat north of Darwin, it was reported yesterday in Washington.

One American plane rammed an enemy fighter and both were destroyed.

U.S. Air Victory

Japanese air raids on Port Moresby, Australia's "Tobruk" in New Guinea, and on other objectives in the Torres Strait (between New Guinea and the Australian mainland) have increased in intensity.

About thirteen fighters and eight bombers were over the Torres Strait and nine heavy bombers were over Port Moresby.

Allied bombers, reinforcing the RAAF, are maintaining continuous raids on Japanese positions in New Guinea, but the arrival of reinforcements is still the most urgent question.

Dead men tell tall tales

Fifty-four Chinese seamen were drowned when they were thrown into the water from their torpedoed ship.

When their bodies were picked up by a Canadian vessel they were re-incarnated. Therefore, re-born in a Canadian ship, they are Canadians, and cannot be deported.

Anyway, that's their argument, and they are pleading it before Canadian port authorities with a vehemence of which their original selves would have been proud.

Canadian authorities, however, are a little suspicious of the theory.

They say that, dead or alive, the Chinese, who have been two months ashore, must go to sea again—or be deported.

U.S. SUB. SINKS CARGO SHIP IN JAP WATERS

A United States submarine has sunk a freighter in Japanese waters, and a tanker has been sunk by undisclosed means in the Philippines area.

Over 150 Japanese ships have been sunk or damaged by United States forces since the Pacific war started.—Associated Press

Sea-air attack on big Italian base

AN unexplained reference to a dramatic combined sea and air daylight attack on Rhodes, Italian-occupied island base in the Mediterranean, was made last night in a Cairo story of an RAF night raid on the island.

An Italian communique yesterday admitted a combined attack, but the RAF report alluded only to the destruction of dispersed aircraft "which would, with the coming of daylight, seek to defend Rhodes against a combined operation."

"Like a Christmas Tree"

Crews of the Wellington medium-heavy bombers returning from the night attack said they met with little opposition.

Anti-aircraft fire against the Wimpeys, as these bombers are called, was negligible as the planes sailed in at intervals to damage the aerodromes and pick off the dispersed aircraft.

A pilot who was over Calato aerodrome reported that he saw Laritza "lit up like a Christmas tree."

Many Fires Burning

"The raid went on till the early hours of the morning, and then bursts of enemy artillery fire were seen, suggesting some opposition to the combined attack which was developing out of sight below," said the report.

Many fires were burning as the RAF raiders left the island. This was the first night visit of the RAF to the Dodecanese Islands for some time.

"Britain, send us help at once"—Burma

WE take it for granted that the British Government realises the gravity of the situation, and is taking immediate steps to send us the largest reinforcements possible to enable our troops to take the offensive and drive the enemy from Burma."

This appeal was made yesterday in Mandalay, threatened by a new Japanese advance, by Sir Paw Tun, Premier of Burma.

"We are determined to fight on," he said. "We have had reverses, but we will never give in to the enemy."

THREE-POWER LABOUR LINK

A favourable answer will be given by the American Federation of Labour to Sir Walter Citrine's invitation to join the Labour movements of Great Britain and Soviet Russia in an international federation to help the war effort of the United Nations.

This answer will be given to Sir Walter when he goes to Washington in the middle of May

Housekeeping news

COAL ● EGGS
all rationed ½d. cheaper

SIX hundredweight of coal (or less) for the three weeks beginning today. That limit, imposed yesterday by the Secretary for Mines, brings the rest of the country into line with London.

Reason—to check the heavy drain on stocks caused by recent severe weather and diversion of supplies to essential war industries.

Generally, delivery of up to 6cwt. of house coal will be permitted only if the occupier of residential premises holds a stock of less than half a ton.

There are variations to the general scheme. Parts of South-East England, supply restricted to 5cwt. Parts of North Midlands, 4cwt.

EGGS will be ½d. each cheaper at the end of this month, when wholesale prices will be reduced to 5s. per long hundred (120 eggs).

Retail prices will be reduced by 6d. a dozen, the new prices being 2s. and 1s. 9d. according to size.

Wholesalers are being instructed to suspend deliveries to retail and multiple shops after close of business on Thursday, March 26.

On the following Saturday the National Egg Distributors' Association, Limited, will begin issuing delivery orders at the new prices, and wholesalers will be authorised to renew deliveries on March 31.

LITVINOV TELLS US TO RISK IT, ATTACK NOW

Litvinov.

NOW is the time for a second front. Inaction will lose the war. Attack may win it.

This was the keynote of a speech made by Comrade Litvinov, Soviet Ambassador to the U.S., in New York last night.

If Hitler's strained armies on the Eastern Front can be weakened by a diversion elsewhere, it will be possible for the Soviet forces to drive the Huns back further—"to Berlin and beyond."

"The more we console ourselves with general statements about the impossibility of losing the war, the further we shall be from looking for realistic ways to victory," said M. Litvinov.

"There may be a much greater actual risk in waiting and doing nothing, in letting slip one opportunity after another.

"Action involving risk has at any rate some chance of success, whereas inaction also involving risk is practically never crowned with success."

"Worth Some Risk"

M. Litvinov said that although the war might drag on through 1943, 1944, and even longer, this did not mean that nothing should be done to try to end it sooner.

"Would not a shortening of the war in itself be worth some risk?" he asked, saying that he feared time to be a treacherous ally, ready to fight for either side.

"In the past nine months, Russia had prevented Hitler from taking any considerable military action on any front, and had given the Allies a breathing-space to accumulate their military forces without undergoing any appreciable loss.

Referring to Germany's tremendous losses on the Eastern front, M. Litvinov said:—

Chance of Victory

"Only think what would have been the power of Germany now if Hitler had maintained intact the armaments with which he began attacking the Soviet Union, plus nine months' output of the factories of Germany, France, Czechoslovakia, Austria and the other occupied countries."

With all the resources of the Soviet Union, plus the assistance of the United States and Britain, it had become possible for the first time to thwart Hitler's plans and drive his armies back.

"We have not driven them far—at the most 200 miles here and there—but it is obvious that if our strength can be increased or—which may be easier to achieve—if the German forces can be split or weakened on the Eastern Front by a diversion elsewhere, it will be possible to push them still further back to the German frontier, to Berlin and beyond.

"The Hitler-hating populations in the countries he has subjected are only waiting for a signal for decisive action.

"And the only signal they will recognise will be a serious defeat for the German Army."

BOMBS FALL ON TURKEY

The German radio said last night, "Three foreign planes have dropped fifteen bombs near Milas (ninety miles south of Smyrna).

"Some houses were destroyed and two people were killed, several others being injured."

Vichy says there were ten dead and twenty injured.

Berlin Boasts

The Premier warned the people of Burma that they must be prepared to endure all kinds of hardships.

He thanked China for the help she has given Burma.

Berlin is boasting that the fall of Mandalay—second most important city of Burma—is expected soon.

Japanese forces, thrusting

Continued on Back Page

AN OLD FAVOURITE

LEMCO
EXTRACT OF BEEF

The Original Concentrated Beef Extract

Still available..

For two generations LEMCO has been a favourite in the kitchen. This concentrated beef extract enriches all meat dishes and is unrivalled for soups and stews. For best results use sparingly—you can also put the attractive Jar on the table and use LEMCO to flavour your soups and stews.

Hope lives again!

occupied countries."

With all the resources of the Soviet Union, plus the assistance of the United States and Britain, it had become possible for the first time to thwart Hitler's plans and drive his armies back.

"We have not driven them far – at the most 200 miles here and there – but it is obvious that if our strength can be increased or – which may be easier to achieve – if the German forces can be split or weakened on the Eastern Front by a diversion elsewhere, it will be possible to push them still further back to the German frontier, to Berlin and beyond.

"The Hitler-hating populations in the countries he has subjected are only waiting for a signal for decisive action.

"And the only signal they will recognise will be a serious defeat for the German Army."

"EXPLAIN THE WAR"

MIGHT it not be a good thing if perambulating public orators and week-end speech-makers were to deny themselves the pleasures of palaver over Easter?

The solemn season invites to meditation – to thought, rather than to talk.

Instead, there is a depressing rumour to the effect that the talkers are to multiply words with the intention of explaining the war.

Explaining it? Or explaining it away?

That is, explaining away defeats by the remark that nobody is to be blamed for them. He who blames anybody else for blunders just shows he doesn't understand war.

Spare us such explanations!

Let the speakers wait till we get a victory plain for all to see. Even then there need be no talk. Victories explain themselves.

THE SPIRIT OF ATTACK
AMONGST the high spots of week-end oratory we come upon this from a subordinate member of the Government:

"The spirit of *attack* is abroad today. Join civil *defence*."

1943, 1944, and even longer, this did not mean that nothing should be done to try to end it sooner.

"Would not a shortening of the war in itself be worth some risk?" he asked, saying that he feared time to be a treacherous ally, ready to fight for either side.

In the past nine months, Russia had prevented Hitler from taking any considerable military action on any front, and had given the Allies a breathing-space to accumulate their military forces without undergoing any appreciable loss.

Referring to Germany's tremendous losses on the Eastern front. M. Litvinov said:

CHANCE OF VICTORY
"Only think what would have been the power of Germany now if Hitler had maintained intact the armaments with which he began attacking the Soviet Union, plus nine months' output of the factories of Germany, France, Czechoslovakia, Austria and the other

Big Shot!!

Philip Zec's cartoon shows Winston Churchill sitting in the sheriff's office watching Lord Beaverbrook dressed as a cowboy pull his gun.

(Italics ours.)

That is just it! If there's a spirit of attack abroad, there must be a spirit of defence at home. Not a spirit of counterattack and of offence.

The old story! Wait for the enemy to strike.

"BARING HIS TEETH"
THIS waiting attitude (according to another M.P.) has become so exasperating to the British lion that he is "baring his teeth for action."

So many of the noble creature's imperial teeth have been extracted of late that he may soon be baring nothing but his gums. What will he do then? "He will roar loud enough to shatter every window in Whitehall."

Since bombs have not roused Whitehall, we doubt if roars will do it. But we entirely agree that the British lion is longing to spring at his enemy, instead of being chased with a tooth-extractor.

24 April **1942**

BEAVERBROOK CALLS FOR INVASION OF EUROPE

"INVADE Europe." This was Lord Beaverbrook's call to the United Nations in a New York speech last night.

"What is the reason for my advocacy of help to Russia?" he

DAILY MIRROR R, Friday, April 24, 1942.
No. 11,969
ONE PENNY
Registered at the G.P.O. as a Newspaper.

Lovat gives his orders

BEAVERBROOK CALLS FOR INVASION OF EUROPE

He must shut 16 shops

SIXTEEN butcher's shops in the Warrington area, owned by William Hollowell, 62, butcher and farmer, of Woodside, Appleton, trading as H. Singleton, are to be closed on June 1 by order of the Ministry of Food.

The Ministry has revoked all retail meat licences held by Hollowell at these shops on the recommendation of the Warrington area Joint Food Control Committee.

This decision follows a number of prosecutions against Hollowell for offences against the rationing and livestock regulations in which he has been fined a total of nearly £200 in the past two years.

"A business which has taken me 52 years to create will now be lost," Mr. Hollowell told the "Daily Mirror" last night.

"I started work at the age of 9 as a half-timer," he said, "and received a shilling a week wages, 3d. for myself.

"I eventually bought a shop and gradually added to this until I now own sixteen shops and a farm."

ELEPHANT BETRAYED A SECRET

A LITTLE old lady in a straw-bonnet-hat smiled as she watched the elephants march by in parade at Chessington Zoo, Surrey, yesterday.

Suddenly a shadow loomed over her head as an elephant waved its trunk. The little straw bonnet soared into the air.

And as they watched an amazed audience saw a wig dangling from the hat in the elephant's trunk.

The little bald head bobbed amid the crowd as the woman, with a shriek of alarm, ran to hide herself from view.

The elephant, Nellie, a star performer at the Chessington Circus, doubled her trunk and, placing wig and bonnet in her mouth, began to chew. Then, with a roar of disgust at the taste, she spat both on to the circus floor and strode angrily on.

A woman clown went to the old lady's assistance, and from a clothing trunk produced an old circus wig and hat.

She offered them to the frightened victim, who seized them gratefully. Then, wearing the circus headgear, she hurried off home—still blushing.

"Carpet-Slippers" Ennis.

'Carpet-slippers' a college 'cop'

THE carpet-slippered Commando officer who, armed with a cosh, "invaded France in comfort" with the Commandos, is 28-year-old ex-Inspector James Ennis, who was one of Lord Trenchard's "boys" from the Hendon Police College.

Former police colleagues in the East End of London—Jock Ennis was stationed at Arbour-square and Limehouse before the war—were not surprised at his latest role.

"Always a good man in a 'rough house,' he more than once proved that he could look after himself during the Fascist and anti - Fascist demonstrations in that part of London.

"Nothing frightened him in this neighbourhood, and he would take any 'rough-house' in his stride," said one of his former colleagues yesterday.

Ennis comes from Glasgow.

BEFORE THE COMMANDO RAID near Boulogne. Major Lord Lovat, who was in charge of the raid, giving orders to his officers just before the Commandos set out. He is the tall figure on the right

Japanese gains on Burma fronts

ALLIED forces are being withdrawn from the Taungdwingyi area in Burma, where for a long time they have held their positions and successfully protected the Allied flank.

This was stated in yesterday's Burma communique.

A Chinese communique yesterday says Chinese forces have withdrawn from Loikaw. Fighting their way through Japanese encirclement, they re-established contact with their main forces further north.

The communique says:

"A Japanese detachment which moved around the Chinese flank and reached the northern outskirts of Loikaw was repulsed by the Chinese, but the Japanese, after receiving reinforcements, again occupied the area north of the city.

"The Chinese garrison succeeded in breaking through the Japanese cordon and re-establishing contact with the Chinese main body.

Planes Aid Attack

"Fighting is in progress in the vicinity of the Pinn River.

"On the railway north of Pyinmana, fighting increased in intensity with Japanese mechanised units led an attack supported by aircraft.

"The Chinese vigorously resisted the attack, and the Japanese left many d'ad on the battlefield.

KILLER SERVED IN DEAD MAN'S SHOP

From JOHN WALTERS
New York, Thursday.

A young bandit shot and killed a Chicago grocery-stores manager today, locked the assistant in the refrigerator, and then calmly served customers for more than an hour.

Smiling, wearing an apron, the bandit sold groceries to scores of customers, chatting about rising prices and the weather.

Then he released the shop assistant, and vanished into the crowded street.

TOKIO RAIDER IN U.S.S.R.

An American bomber has landed on Soviet territory in the Far East. The crew, who were interned, declared they had taken part in bombing Tokio and had lost their way, said Moscow radio last night.

"INVADE Europe." This was Lord Beaverbrook's call to the United Nations in a New York speech last night.

"What is the reason for my advocacy of help to Russia?" he asked. "It is the knowledge that Russia may settle the war for us in 1942. By holding the Germans in check, possibly even by defeating them, the Russians may be the means of bringing the whole Axis structure down.

"This is a chance to bring the war to an end here and now. But if the Russians are defeated and driven out of the war, never will such a chance come to us again.

"Strike out to help Russia. Strike out violently. Strike even recklessly. In any case, such blows will be our contribution to the Russian battle front.

"How admirably Britain is now equipped in weapons of war for directing an attack on Germany I well know . . . our tank production has been doubled in the last six months. And our output of guns of two-pounder calibre and over exceeds 35,000 a year.

"Master of Tactics"

"We know the Russians kill more Germans every day than all the Allies put together. Russia is the fighting front. That is the opportunity, the chance to bring Germans to battle.

"I believe in the Russian system which holds to the faith that the best form of defence is attack.

"Britain should imitate Russia's spirit of attack by establishing somewhere along the 2,000-mile occupied coast line a second front.

"Ever since my journey to Russia in October last I have been in favour of a second front. British and American supply missions at that time provided our ally with aircraft and tanks, A.A. guns and anti-tank guns. And some short-sighted people complained that we did wrong to put weapons in the hands of Communists.

"I don't understand the complaint. Communism under Stalin has produced the most valiant fighting army in Europe. Communism under Stalin has won the applause and admiration of all Western nations.

"Communism under Stalin has produced the best generals in this war.

"Persecution of Christianity? Not so. There is no religious persecution. The church doors are open. There is complete freedom to practise religion just as there is complete freedom to reject it.

"Racial persecution? Not at

Continued on Back Page

Joining de Gaulle

The five members of the Vichy Embassy in Washington who resigned on Wednesday have offered their services to General de Gaulle.

The Vichy Government, cables John Walters, will be greatly embarrassed by the transfer of one of the staff, Charles Benoit, for he was director of the Embassy code room.

WOMEN WAR WORKERS' RISE

MANY thousands of women war workers are to get increases in pay.

Negotiations have been concluded by the Transport and General Workers' Union and the National Union of General and Municipal Workers covering pay for "manually employed" women in Government factories.

The result is that women employed in certain Royal Ordnance factories will be paid on the same basis as production and process workers.

The decision affects workers in explosive factories and most of the engineering factories, but not filling factories.

The increases in rates are of varying amounts, rising by as much as 13s. a week.

Those who will benefit, numbering many thousands, include women on labour duties, inspection work and in stores.

Canteen workers, telephone operators and office cleaners are now included.

Women on semi-skilled work other than production or process jobs will receive the same "lead" rates for efficiency as men.

"The two unions have been deeply concerned over the delay in dealing with the rates of pay for women employed by various Government departments," said a union official.

J.C. Walker's cartoon refers to the appointment of Lord Beaverbrook to the post of Minister of Supply in June 1941.

"Lord Beaverbrook will now be our Mr. Nelson."—The Prime Minister.

The Treaty

TREATY OF ALLIANCE IN THE WAR AGAINST HITLERITE GERMANY AND HER ASSOCIATES IN EUROPE AND OF COLLABORATION AND MUTUAL ASSISTANCE THEREAFTER CONCLUDED BETWEEN THE UNION OF SOVIET SOCIALIST REPUBLICS AND THE UNITED KINGDOM OF GREAT BRITAIN AND NORTHERN IRELAND. LONDON, MAY 26, 1942.

PART I

Article I.—In virtue of the alliance established between the United Kingdom and the Union of Soviet Socialist Republics the High Contracting Parties mutually undertake to afford one another military and other assistance and support of all kinds in the war against Germany and all those States which are associated with her in acts of aggression in Europe.

Article II.—The High Contracting Parties undertake ***not to enter into any negotiations with the Hitlerite Government or any other Government in Germany that does not clearly renounce all aggressive intentions, and not to negotiate or conclude except by mutual consent any armistice or peace treaty with Germany or any other State associated with her in acts of aggression in Europe.***

PART II

Article III.—(1) The High Contracting Parties declare their desire to unite with other like-minded States in adopting proposals for common action to preserve peace and resist aggression in the post-war period.

(2) Pending the adoption of such proposals, they will after the termination of hostilities take all the measures in their power to render impossible a repetition of aggression and violation of the peace by Germany or any of the States associated with her in acts of aggression in Europe.

Mutual Help

Article IV.—Should one of the High Contracting Parties during the post-war period become involved in hostilities with Germany or any of the States mentioned in Article III (2) in consequence of an attack by that State against that Party, the other High Contracting Party will at once give to the Contracting Party so involved in hostilities all the military and other support and assistance in his power.

This Article shall remain in force until the High Contracting Parties, by mutual agreement, shall recognise that it is superseded by the adoption of the proposals contemplated in Article III (1). In default of the adoption of such proposals, it shall remain in force for a period of twenty years, and thereafter until terminated by either High Contracting Party as provided in Article VIII.

No Interference

Article V.—The High Contracting Parties, having regard to the interests of the security of each of them, agree to work together in close and friendly collaboration after the re-establishment of peace for the organisation of security and economic prosperity in Europe. They will take into account the interests of the United Nations in these objects, and they will act in accordance with the two principles of not seeking territorial aggrandisement for themselves and of non-interference in the internal affairs of other States.

Article VI.—The High Contracting Parties agree to render one another all possible economic assistance after the war.

Article VII.—Each High Contracting Party undertakes not to conclude any alliance and not to take part in any coalition directed against the other High Contracting Party.

Article VIII.—The present Treaty is subject to ratification in the shortest possible time and the instruments of ratification shall be exchanged in Moscow as soon as possible.

It comes into force immediately on the exchange of the instruments of ratification and shall thereupon replace the Agreement between the Government of the Union of Soviet Socialist Republics and his Majesty's Government in the United Kingdom, signed at Moscow on July 12, 1941.

Part I of the present Treaty shall remain in force until the re-establishment of peace between the High Contracting Parties and Germany and the Powers associated with her in acts of aggression in Europe.

To Continue

Part II of the present Treaty shall remain in force for a period of twenty years. Thereafter, unless twelve months' notice has been given by either Party to terminate the Treaty at the end of the said period of twenty years, it shall continue in force until twelve months after either High Contracting Party shall have given notice to the other in writing of his intention to terminate it.

In witness whereof the above-named *Plenipotentiaries* have signed the present Treaty and have affixed thereto their seals.

Done in duplicate in London on May 26, 1942, in the English and Russian languages, both texts being equally authentic.

ANTHONY EDEN.
V. MOLOTOV

TEXT OF MESSAGE FROM HIS MAJESTY THE KING TO M. KALININ, CHAIRMAN OF THE PRESIDIUM OF THE SUPREME COUNCIL OF THE U.S.S.R.

I cannot let this occasion pass without expressing to you, Mr. President, my gratification at the signature which has taken place this day of our Treaty of Alliance.

This Treaty consecrates the efforts of our two countries in the hard and bitter struggle they are waging, and pledges them to wholehearted co-operation and mutual support in the years that will follow our victory.

World Benefit

I like to believe that you, Mr. President, welcome it as sincerely as I do myself, and that you share my confidence that its effect will be to the benefit not only of our two countries but of all the world.

TEXT OF MESSAGE IN REPLY FROM M. KALININ TO HIS MAJESTY THE KING.

I fully share the satisfaction expressed by Your Majesty at the signing of the Treaty of Alliance between our countries.

I am sure that the treaty now signed will consolidate yet further the fighting Alliance of our countries in their stern and uncompromising struggle against the common enemy and will ensure cordial co-operation and mutual assistance in the years following victory.

I welcome the treaty as sincerely as does Your Majesty, and express the conviction that this treaty will be of benefit not only to our two countries but to all the world.

TEXT OF SPEECH BY MR. ANTHONY EDEN, SECRETARY OF STATE FOR FOREIGN AFFAIRS, ON THE OCCASION OF THE SIGNATURE OF THE TREATY.

On behalf of His Majesty's Government in the United Kingdom, I welcome you, M. Molotov, as Foreign Secretary of the Union of Soviet Socialist Republics.

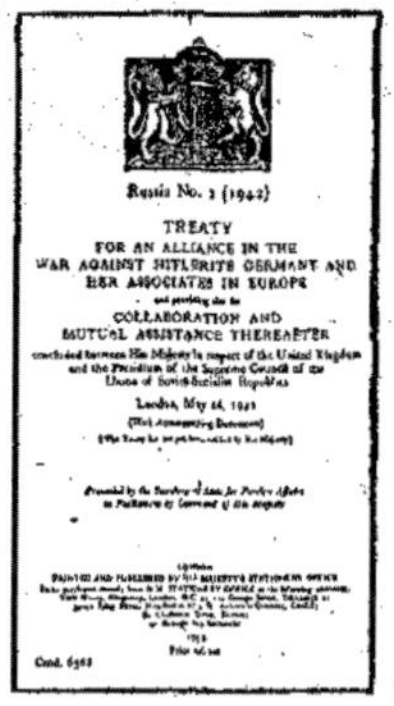

Russia No. 1 (1942)
TREATY
FOR AN ALLIANCE IN THE WAR AGAINST HITLERITE GERMANY AND HER ASSOCIATES IN EUROPE
COLLABORATION AND MUTUAL ASSISTANCE THEREAFTER
London, May 26, 1942
Cmd. 6368

We are met in a world at war, when our two countries are together at grips with the common enemy. Under the impact of war we have found that understanding which escaped us in the uneasy years of peace. *The treaty which we have just signed* engages us to continue the struggle together until the victory be won. On behalf of my colleagues I give you the pledge that there will be no wavering in this endeavour on the part of the Government or people of these islands

Maisky Praised

Such, then, is the first chapter of our task, the overthrow of Hitler and the destruction of all that his regime stands for. But there is a second chapter also to our Treaty. One day the war will end. One day the common enemy will be defeated and there will be peace again. We must see to it that this time peace endures. In the Treaty which we have signed we pledge ourselves to work together for this purpose.

Never before in the history of our two countries has our association been so close, or our mutual pledge for the future so complete. This is surely a happy augury. There is nothing exclusive in our agreement. We are seeking peace and security not only for our two countries, but for *all the United Nations*. But understanding between us is one of the foundations of peace, not for us alone, but for the world. We have signed our Treaty, and part of the work is behind us.

I would like to say now, M. Molotov, how much we have *valued the statesmanship* and insight which you have shown in our negotiations. I would like, too, to thank M. Maisky, your Ambassador, who has done so much in his years here to build a bridge between our two countries

Peace to Build

Part of the work is behind us. But the greater part yet lies ahead. There is the war to win. There is the peace to build. Neither of these tasks is for ourselves alone. You yourself, M. Molotov, are leaving our shores for the United States. Upon the co-operation of the Soviet Union, the United States of America and the British Commonwealth the future of mankind will largely depend. We thank you for your work with us here and we wish you well upon your journey.

TEXT OF SPEECH MADE BY M. MOLOTOV, PEOPLE'S COMMISSAR FOR FOREIGN AFFAIRS, ON THE OCCASION OF THE SIGNATURE OF THE TREATY.

Mr. Churchill, Gentlemen,—The Treaty between the Union of Soviet Socialist Republics and Great Britain of alliance in the war against Hitlerite Germany and her accomplices in Europe, and of co-operation and mutual assistance after the war, which I have just had the honour to sign in the name of the Government of the U.S.S.R., represents an important political landmark in the development of relations between Great Britain and the Soviet Union.

The Treaty between us is essential not only to the peoples of the U.S.S.R. and Great Britain, but also to the peoples of other countries. Permit me to express my confidence that all peoples who have experienced the aggression of the German-Fascist Imperialists or whose freedom and honour have been threatened, and may still be threatened, by the Hitlerite band of robbers, oppressors and ravishers—all these will express their satisfaction at the conclusion of this historic Treaty.

Common Action

Our allies all over the world will share with us the warmest feelings of satisfaction. Our Treaty is indispensable in order the more quickly to ensure the destruction of Hitlerite Germany and to attain our desired aim — victory.

The present treaty also determines the common line of action of the Soviet Union and Great Britain after the war. The fact that this treaty operates for a period of twenty years, and is based on mutual military and economic assistance against possible further aggression on the part of Germany and is intended to ensure the security and economic well-being of the peoples of Europe, speaks for itself.

Hitler and his accomplices in their blood-stained robbery in Europe will now feel more than ever that the united forces of their adversaries have been rallied and strengthened. So much the better for us, for our peoples, for our common cause.

This treaty signifies and contains much more than the Anglo-Soviet agreement of last year

The New Stage

The treaty of May 26, 1942, marks a new and important stage in the development of Anglo-Soviet relations on a basis of alliance and mutual military assistance against our common and irreconcilable foe, both of today and of the future, in Europe. It provides the desired basis for joint action after the war, thus greatly adding to its importance.

It is still further necessary to emphasise that what relates to the present day in this treaty is already successfully being realised and carried into effect. Such a treaty will be welcomed with great satisfaction by the masses of the Soviet Union, where, under the direction of their great Leader and Supreme Commander, J. V. Stalin, the Red Army is carrying on a heroic struggle against the German invaders, confident in the belief that the time is not far distant when our just cause will achieve full victory

Soviet Thanks

Please accept, Mr. Prime Minister Churchill and Mr. Secretary Eden, to whom the present treaty owes so much, my sincere gratitude for the active part you have taken at all stages.

I express my sincere personal gratitude to His Majesty's Government for the hospitality shown to me as the representative of the Government of the U.S.S.R.

In conclusion, I wish to express my firm conviction that the treaty which has been signed today well serves the cause of our victory, the cause of the great future of our two peoples.

TODAY
RADI

asked. "It is the knowledge that Russia may settle the war for us in 1942. By holding the Germans in check, possibly even by defeating them, the Russians may be the means of bringing the whole Axis structure down.

"This is a chance to bring the war to an end here and now. But if the Russians are defeated and driven out of the war, never will such a chance come to us again.

"Strike out to help Russia. Strike out violently. Strike even recklessly. In any case, such blows will be our contribution to the Russian battle front.

"How admirably Britain is now equipped in weapons of war for directing an attack on Germany I well know . . . our tank production has been doubled in the last six months. And our output of guns of two-pounder calibre and over exceeds 35,000 a year."

"MASTER OF TACTICS"

"We know the Russians kill more Germans every day than all the Allies put together. Russia is the fighting front. That is the opportunity, the chance to bring Germans to battle.

"I believe in the Russian system which holds to the faith that the best form of defence is attack.

"Britain should imitate Russia's spirit of attack by establishing somewhere along the 2,000-mile occupied coastline a second front.

"Ever since my journey to Russia in October last I have been in favour of a second front. British and American supply missions at that time provided our ally with aircraft and tanks, A.A. guns and anti-tank guns. And some short-sighted people complained that we did wrong to put weapons in the hands of Communists.

"I don't understand the complaint. Communism under Stalin has produced the most valiant fighting army in Europe. Communism under Stalin has won the applause and admiration of all Western nations.

"Communism under Stalin has produced the best generals in this war.

"Persecution of Christianity? Not so. There is no religious persecution. The church doors are open. There is complete freedom to practise religion just as there is complete freedom to reject it.

"Racial persecution? Not at all. Jews live like other men. There are many races in the Soviet Union and not even a colour bar.

"Political purges? Of course. But it is now clear that men who were shot down would have betrayed Russia to her German enemy."

Lord Beaverbrook described Mr. Churchill as a "great Crusader of modern times."

No thought of compromise ever entered his head, even in the darkest hours.

Mr. Churchill was the embodiment of the spirit of Britain today – dogged, grim, undaunted.

Giving an account of his conversations in Washington, General Sikorski told the Polish National Council in London yesterday that he said to Mr. Roosevelt:

"The Nazis are unable to recreate the former Hitlerite divisions which won lightning victories.

"The decisive factor will undoubtedly be great battles on the European continent.

"The Allies must resolutely and at all costs strive to create a second front in Europe."

SURPRISE ATTACK

WHAT is it that so greatly encourages our people in the series of Commando raids upon the French coast; as also in our air raids upon Western Germany?

Obviously, the welcome element of surprise, the spirit of daring, the vigour of offensive action.

Defence, withdrawal, retreat, must be discouraging words in war; though they have to be heard stoically.

Good words, cancelling all sense of frustration and impatience are attack, aggression, charge the enemy, worry him, keep him guessing, and give him an occasional surprise.

The stimulating results on morale may be much greater than the tactical achievement.

Non-stop Hammer and Schickle!

Sir Stafford Cripps, the British Ambassador to the Soviet Union, signs the agreement between the two countries to join together in the war against Germany. Directly behind him at the meeting in Moscow in July 1941 is Joseph Stalin.

20-YEAR PACT WITH RUSSIA MEANS A SECOND FRONT IN 1942

POST-WAR ARMS AID PLANNING PEACE
By OUR POLITICAL CORRESPONDENT

BRITAIN and Russia have signed a "peace and war" Treaty of mutual assistance to last for twenty years.

A crowded House of Commons cheered again and again when Mr. Anthony Eden made this announcement last night. M. Molotov, Russia's Foreign Minister, Mr. Eden revealed, has been in London, in Washington, and back again in London without a word of his journeyings reaching the public in either country.

But more than the signing of one of the most important treaties in world history was accomplished.

Full understanding was reached between the leaders of both countries with regard to the "urgent task of creating a second front in Europe in 1942."

Mr. Eden seemed to stress the date in his speech – and the House roared its approval.

In Washington, M. Molotov discussed the same matter with President Roosevelt and arrived at a complete agreement with him.

STAFF CHIEFS AT TALKS

In London the British Chiefs of Staff took part in the discussions regarding a second front this year, most of the conversations being carried on at Chequers, the Prime Minister's country house.

The complete harmony in which agreement was reached on all points is shown by the fact that M. Molotov reached here on May 20, after a hazardous journey, delayed considerably by bad weather, and had left for Washington exactly seven days later.

The Treaty had been signed the day before, and he flew the Atlantic with the text of it in his pocket to show to President Roosevelt.

There were further talks on his return to London, when he bore with him the American Government's approval of all that had been decided. Now he is back in Moscow to report to M. Stalin on the outstanding success of his mission.

I understand that although they are not mentioned in the Treaty, the thorny problem of the western frontiers was discussed at length and appreciable progress, towards which the Poles played a part, was made in laying the foundation for a future settlement.

The Pact . . . can be briefly summed up as follows:

Russia and Britain agree to give mutual assistance until peace is reached and during the post-war period if attacked by Germany or any of her European associates, this to last for twenty years or until ended by mutual agreement.

They agree to collaborate for a peaceful settlement of Europe on the basis of the Atlantic Charter.

Each side pledges itself not to make a separate peace, and announces that it has no territorial ambitions.

In his speech, Mr. Eden paid tribute to the work of the Soviet Ambassador, M. Maisky, towards bringing the two countries closer.

The House responded with a burst of cheering that left no doubt as to their feelings. In the Ambassadors' Gallery sat M. Maisky and his eyes beamed with pleasure. For once he did not trouble to hide his feelings.

SURPRISE FOR M.P.S

Never, perhaps, has the House heard a better deserved tribute.

Mr. Eden's announcement of the Treaty took many M.P.s by surprise. Some had hurried home at the end of the coal debate and so missed the dramatic climax to the Parliamentary day.

Just when the House should have been adjourning Mr. Eden sipped a glass of water and put a manuscript on the dispatch box.

There was a flutter in the galleries, Mrs. Eden slipped quietly into a seat and was joined by Mrs. Churchill, Lady Anderson, Mrs. Gwilym Lloyd George and Mme. Maisky. Nearby sat Miss Mary Churchill. Mr. Winant, U.S. Ambassador, was with M. Maisky.

NO SECRET CLAUSES

Mr. Eden, after outlining the terms of the Treaty, said it contained a ratification clause, and both Governments were anxious it should come into force as soon as possible.

There were cheers when he assured Mr. Arthur Greenwood that there were no secret clauses or commitments between Britain and Russia.

Unexpectedly, Mr. Lloyd George rose. As one who strove for twenty years to bring about an understanding with Russia, he congratulated the Government, and said that if the pact had been signed years ago blunders would have been avoided and this war would never have been fought.

A communiqué issued later by the Foreign Office said: "Full understanding was reached between the two parties with regard to the urgent tasks of creating a second front in Europe in 1942."

CHURCHILL'S THANKS TO STALIN

"WE are very grateful to you for helping us to overcome difficulties we had with the Treaty."

This is part of a message from Mr. Churchill to Stalin, quoted by Moscow radio last night.

"I am convinced," the message continued, "that from now on the three Great Powers will be able to march step by step together towards whatever is expected of them.

"I had great pleasure in meeting M. Molotov, and we have done much together to remove the obstacles between our two countries.

"As we have pledged ourselves to remain friends and allies for the next twenty years, I am taking this opportunity of sending you my best wishes, and expressing my conviction that victory will be ours."

This was Stalin's reply:

"I am grateful to you for your good wishes."

"GREAT SIGNIFICANCE"

"I am convinced this Treaty will be of great significance in the further strengthening of the friendly relations between the Soviet Union and Great Britain, as well as between our countries and the U.S., and that it will secure the close collaboration of our countries after the victorious conclusion of the war.

"May I ask you to accept my sincere good wishes, and my expression of my firm belief in our common complete victory."

M. MOLOTOV'S TIMETABLE

Here is the timetable of M. Molotov's mission:

May 20. – Arrived in England.
May 21. – First conversations.
May 25. – Agreement reached.
May 26. – Agreement signed. M. Molotov left London.
May 29. – Arrived in America.
June 4. – Left America.

THEY DIDN'T KNOW IT WAS MOLOTOV

M. Molotov arrived by special train at a tiny English station. No one knew he was coming. No one recognised him when he came. This is the story of the village that missed its Big Day.

By E. H. CHRISTIAN (Daily Mirror Reporter)

A TINY country station in the damp coolness of the evening . . . a train drew in and stopped . . . a world-famous diplomat alighted.

There were no cheering crowds. There were no ceremonial presentations.

That is how M. Molotov, Russian Foreign Minister, arrived.

I was the only journalist present to see this great occasion. It was a world scoop which I could not use.

M. Molotov arrived from the north in a seven-coach special train. He came to a station on the outskirts of London, set in fields, with a few houses in the nearby village.

George, the station master, and his one porter were the staff to greet this "special". A contingent of Air Force men and police arrived well before the train was due.

They had not long to wait, for the train was ahead of schedule.

A number of large cars arrived later, bearing Mr. Eden, M. Maisky, and other members of the welcoming party.

Even Anthony Eden's well-known face attracted no crowd. The only members of the public present, apart from the *Daily Mirror* photographer and myself, were two village women.

They were so concerned with catching their train that they had no thought for the identity or importance of the visitor.

NO CEREMONY

The meeting of M. Molotov and the welcoming party was without ceremony.

The Foreign Commissar, hatless, and dressed in a grey suit, stepped from the train and shook hands with Mr. Eden, M. Maisky, and other officials, smiling broadly. Mr. Eden also seemed in excellent spirits.

The greetings on the platform were brief. A faint drizzle sprayed the party as it straggled up the incline from the station to the road. Mr. Eden led the way, with M. Molotov and M. Maisky following side by side.

While waiting for the cars to be brought up, M. Molotov stood, hatless, talking to his Ambassador and Mr. Eden. The informality was out of keeping with the importance of the occasion.

DAY OF RUMOURS

Filled with officials, the first car moved forward. M. Molotov and M. Maisky entered the second car with two of their staff. They shook hands again as they parted from Mr. Eden.

"Till tomorrow, then," said our Foreign Secretary, as he smiled goodbye.

Within half an hour the occasion was over. The village had missed its big moment. George was once again issuing tickets.

Next morning the village buzzed with rumours about the visitor. They ranged from Stalin to Roosevelt.

But until the villagers read this story they will not know for certain his identity.

SECOND FRONT THRILLS U.S.

Announcement of the plans for a second front in 1942 has thrilled America, says Reuter from Washington.

The implication is that shipping difficulties will not be allowed to stand in the way.

It is also assumed the forthcoming big air raids by British and American forces will constitute the preliminary action.

News of the Anglo-Soviet Treaty was given to Russia in an announcement broadcast by all Soviet radio stations, whose programmes were interrupted.

BRITAIN AND RUSSIA

THE terms of the treaty with Russia, announced by Mr. Eden in the House of Commons yesterday afternoon, confirm our alliance with her during the war against Germany. But they do much more than that.

They look beyond the war to the difficult succeeding stages of armistice and peace, of salvage and recovery.

They prolong the present alliance into the post-war period. Most necessarily! For what nation, seeking for security against sudden aggression, can ever trust Germany again?

For years the watch and ward must be close and continuous. It must be maintained here in war-wasted Europe. We cannot rely on far distant help. It follows that, though the principles of the Atlantic Charter are invoked in this solemn new agreement, the *military* task of keeping guard over Germany must fall upon ourselves and our allies in Europe – upon those who have kept fighting on the two fronts, east and west; though ultimately we must hope also for the collaboration of a restored Free France.

So ends, we trust, all rumour and fear concerning separate plans, dissociations, betrayals of the common cause – rumours spread no doubt by "enemy action." Our people will rejoice at the news that friendship with Russia, which might have prevented the war, will now be confirmed in the determination to prevent another.

Mr. Eden gave further cause for hope when he spoke of the "full understanding" that had been reached with regard to the urgent task of creating a second front in Europe in 1942.

A full understanding. Not *clamour*! Excellent!

CHURCHILL TO STALIN: I HAD TO SPEAK MY MIND: MOSCOW TALKS CORDIAL

If M. Stalin and Mr. Churchill have reached agreement on a Second Front no indication was given in the short communiqué issued last night following the announcement of their four-day conference in Moscow last week.

Churchill flew to Moscow – for part of the way in a Liberator bomber – at Stalin's invitation, and decisions were reached towards the most complete co-ordination for grand strategy and the future relations of all the United Nations.

In a cable sent to Stalin last night, Churchill said:

"I take the opportunity to thank you for your friendly attitude and hospitality.

"I am highly satisfied that I have visited Moscow.

"FIRST, BECAUSE IT WAS MY DUTY TO SPEAK MY MIND.

"SECONDLY, BECAUSE I AM SURE THAT OUR CONTACT WILL BE USEFUL FOR OUR COMMON CAUSE.

"Please convey my regards to M. Molotov."

Before leaving Moscow the Premier had said:

"We are fully determined, whatever sufferings and difficulties lie ahead of us, to continue the struggle hand in hand with our comrades and brothers until the last remnants of the Hitler regime have turned to dust and remain in our memories as a warning and example for the future."

⬧ Winston Churchill meets Joseph Stalin, the Soviet dictator, for the first time as the two leaders hold talks in Moscow in August 1942.

31

D for Dieppe Day

For all the talk, there was one burst of Allied action in Western Europe. It came on 19 August 1942. Vice-Admiral Louis Mountbatten, Chief of Combined Operations, was keen to test his forces against real opposition, so devised and won approval for a raid on a French port heavily defended by the occupying German army. Some 6,000 Allied troops – 5,000 of them Canadian, the rest British – took part in the mission. Three thousand Allied servicemen were killed in a single day in a disastrous defeat, although contemporary reports put a more positive spin on events. Lessons would have to be learned, and tactics greatly improved, before Allied soldiers would once again be put on French beaches.

◀ An Allied tank on the beach at Dieppe during the ill-fated operation in August 1942.

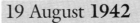

19 August **1942**

MOSCOW'S VERDICT ON TALKS

From MARION SINCLAIR,
Moscow, Tuesday

ALL this morning's Moscow papers have a big front page photograph of Stalin, Churchill and Averell Harriman sitting on a sofa together, smiling.

There are editorials in most papers, notably *Pravda* and *Izvestia*, but significantly perhaps none in the Red Army paper *Red Star*, which may reflect the "not words but deeds" attitude of the Red Army towards us.

Pravda's editorial is little more than a cautious re-write of the communiqué. *Izvestia* is warmer, stressing the phrase in the communiqué: "To carry on with all power and energy."

SECOND FRONT CALL

The paper adds: "That is precisely what wide sections of British and American opinion are expecting, as shown by their urgent demand for active operations by British and U.S. forces in Europe."

All Russian papers continue to give quotations from the British Press demanding a second front.

Pravda published a bitter cartoon by Yeflmov called "On the coast-line," showing a dummy Nazi attached to a gramophone inside a pillbox shouting: "Our fortifications are impregnable. Just you dare to stick your nose in."

The Russians are greatly cheered by Churchill's visit, but now the Premier has gone, Russian opinion is waiting anxiously for the sequel.

20 August **1942**

◀ Allied soldiers are captured by German forces during the raid on Dieppe.

TANKS IN ALL DAY ATTACK IN BATTLE OF DIEPPE

THE Battle of Dieppe was still in full swing late yesterday afternoon. Between 3.15 and 3.45 very heavy explosions shook buildings on this side of the Channel.

Air activity continued with big forces of our fighters – all heading in the Dieppe direction – repeatedly roaring out across the Channel.

The *Daily Mirror* understands that Britain's latest "invasion" barges were used in the landings.

TROOPS OF FOUR NATIONS WERE LANDED

While combined operations were in progress, two squadrons of Flying Fortress bombers of the U.S. Army Air Corps, escorted by fighters of the RAF and Royal Canadian Air Force, made a high level attack on the enemy fighter base at Abbeville, north-east of Dieppe.

Many bursts were seen on buildings, runways and dispersal areas and fires were started. All the bombers returned safely.

Troops of four nations – British, Canadian, United States and Fighting French – co-operated with the Royal Navy and Royal Air Force in the attack at Dieppe, which involved the landing of tanks, and was officially stated last night to have achieved some of its objects.

"Heavy fighting is proceeding," announced yesterday afternoon's combined operations headquarters communiqué, which stated:

"The troops taking part in the raid on the Dieppe area have landed at all the points selected.

"Heavy opposition was encountered in some places, and on the left flank one landing party was initially repulsed, but re-formed and later carried the beach by assault.

"The troops on the right flank having achieved their objective, which included the complete destruction of a six-gun battery and ammunition dump, have now been re-embarked.

"In the centre tanks were landed and heavy fighting is proceeding.

"The military forces consist mainly of Canadian troops. Also taking part are British Special Service troops, a detachment from

a United States Ranger Battalion, and a small contingent of Fighting French.

"These forces were carried and escorted by units of the Royal Navy.

"Air support as protection on a large scale is being provided by bomber and fighter aircraft of the RAF in face of considerable opposition."

Last night the sky over Dieppe was stained with smoke from the fires started by the raiders.

An earlier combined operations headquarters communiqué stated:

"A raid was launched in the early hours of today on the Dieppe area of enemy-occupied France.

"The operation is still in progress and a further communiqué will be issued when fuller reports are available.

"Meanwhile the French people are being advised by wireless broadcasts that this raid is not an invasion."

The Royal Air Force provided an air "umbrella" for the Forces engaged in the attack, which was the first daylight Commando raid on France.

There was a constant procession of aircraft towards the French coast.

Seldom have the people of South-East England, accustomed as they are to the frequent passage of massed aerial squadrons, heard so much sustained thrumming of planes.

The heavy low note of the big bombers remained constant for a long time.

"A roar of giant planes was heard," a South Coast resident declared. "They could not be seen, but there was no mistaking the significance of the noise."

It is now obvious from the communiqués that the engagement is of greater dimensions than any of the raids so far undertaken.

The fact that tanks are for the first time mentioned as being employed in operations of this nature is a development of the greatest importance.

It is not possible yet to make any valuable assessment of success, but the destruction of a six-gun battery is already a solid achievement.

◀ Allied tanks land on the beach at Dieppe.

OUR OBJECT MORE THAN DESTRUCTION

The new operations show that this increased defensive power has already been matched by a heavier striking force.

The combined operations communiqué discloses an ambitious departure in carrying out a Commando raid of this kind in broad daylight, writes a military correspondent.

Our Commando troops could not stay on shore in broad daylight unless they were in considerable strength, and they must be protected by a large force of our aircraft.

It is probable that our object must be the destruction of some important military installation, but there will be more in it than that, for very valuable information as to the strength of the enemy's defences and the location of his units on the coast will be obtained.

With the second front a topical subject, especially since Mr. Churchill's conference with Stalin in Moscow, the raid on Dieppe takes on more than usual significance.

⬥ Preparation for the raid on Dieppe included surveillance photographs taken by low-flying aircraft.

TIME TABLE OF RAID

HERE is a minute-to-minute timetable showing how news of the Commando operation was received in London:

7.00: Combined Operations headquarters issued the first communiqué.
7.30: French people warned by B.B.C. that "This is no invasion."
8.12: Radio Paris went off the air.
8.30: B.B.C. repeated its warning to France, adding that the raid was still in progress.
10.43: Deutschlandsender German long-wave station broadcast code signals. German People Told.

11.15: B.B.C. again broadcast warning to French people, this time attributing it to "an official spokesman of the British Government."
11.35: German News Agency gave Germany its first news of the raid, saying the British force included tanks.
12.20: German News Agency claimed that part of British landing forces had been wiped out and that a counter-attack was in progress.
1.06: Combined Operations headquarters issued a further communiqué on progress of operations.
1.10: U.S. Army headquarters, European centre of operations, issued a communiqué.

⬥ Vice-Admiral Lord Louis Mountbatten, Chief of Combined Operations and architect of the Dieppe raid, discusses a training exercise with troops a month before the operation was launched.

Hors d'oeuvre! *The reconnaissance in force on Dieppe gave morale a great lift, taught us valuable lessons, and gave a foretaste of the D-Days to come.*

(August 8, 1942)

ALL WANTED TO GO

SPECIALLY selected American task troops, chosen from an "avalanche of volunteers" from various branches of the Army, have been in training for some time with the Commandos, it was announced yesterday.

These special task troops make up with United States "Ranger Battalions," some of which took part in yesterday's raid.

United States officers have for some time been serving on the staff of the Chief of Combined Operations, Vice-Admiral Lord Louis Mountbatten.

BRITISH TANKS "SHOT UP" CLAIM

Here is an enemy version of the Dieppe raid. It was issued by the German news agency:

"The attack was delivered west and east of Dieppe against the town and harbour.

"The raiding force was heavily engaged with the defenders.

"The attack met with immediate resistance and part of the British landing force has already been wiped out.

"A number of British tanks were shot up and several transport ships sunk or set on fire before reaching the coast.

"A counter-attack for the final mopping up of the landing force is in progress.

"The number of British killed already amounts to some hundreds, and a number of prisoners have been taken.

"German troops are advancing according to plan, and the British losses in men and material increase hourly."

21 August 1942

◄ The raid on Dieppe taught the Allies valuable lessons about landing in occupied France, but at great cost.

DIEPPE: THIS IS WHAT HAPPENED

THE full story can now be told of the Dieppe battle. Our forces landed at five points – at Berneval and Puits, east of Dieppe, on Dieppe beach itself, and at two points near Varengville, west of Dieppe.

Objectives of the Berneval and Varengville landings were to silence two enemy batteries covering the approaches to Dieppe.

By a thousand-to-one chance the attack at Berneval was discovered before it could be launched and was defeated.

Of the surviving Commandos who dropped back to the beach for re-embarkation, many were wounded and dying.

This initial failure was a setback felt throughout the whole operation and was partly responsible for later difficulties.

At Puits Canadian troops were beaten back at their first rush, but they then re-formed and swept through.

Meanwhile at Varengville Commandos making the double attack on the second Hun battery captured and destroyed the guns with relatively light losses and soon afterwards were withdrawn.

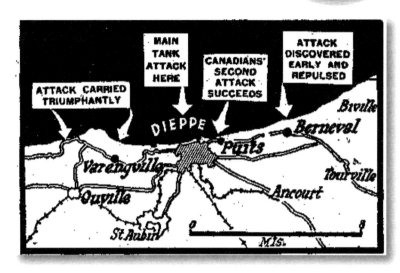

Lord Lovat led this attack, which ended in an all-in battle during which all the enemy gunners were either killed or taken prisoner.

RACECOURSE CAPTURED

When the main landings were made on Dieppe beach, under cover of naval gunfire, tanks helped to clear the way into the town.

During the battle Dieppe racecourse was captured and set up as an emergency landing ground.

One pilot who used it destroyed his machine and returned to England with the ground forces.

An enemy patrol was the cause of the Berneval failure.

The result was that not only were the Commandos' craft severely damaged by German flak ships and E-boats, who held their fire until the landing craft were only about 200 yards away, but, much more important, warning was given to the Germans defending the coastal battery, the landing's objective.

So, when the Commandos landed on the assignment beach, they simply walked into a curtain of fire. It came from every small arm the enemy could muster.

The defenders even trained their anti-aircraft guns on the beach.

Against this rain of death the Commandos, who had needed some measure of surprise, spent themselves in vain – and the battery went on firing.

The Royal Regiment of Canada were detailed to make the Puits landing – a flanking attack to cover the Dieppe beach operations.

E-BOATS ATTACK

About fifty minutes before we were due to hit the beach a flare arched above the Channel (said one correspondent with the Canadians).

Then E-boats appeared close by and kept up a running attack for twenty minutes.

Destroyers sent them scurrying off. Black smoke then billowed out to conceal us from the shore defences.

Already some Royals were landing at Puits as we headed for the beach.

To one side fighter planes hopped in at sea level to blast with cannon and machine-guns the hotels and buildings full of Germans on Dieppe esplanade.

By the time our boat touched the beach it was dotted with the fallen forms of men in battledress. The Royals ahead of us had been cut down as they stormed the slope.

Bursts of yellow tracers from German machine-guns made a veritable curtain about our boat. The Royals beside me fired back with everything they had.

TORRENT OF FIRE

The Germans held a couple of houses near the top of the slope and occupied some strong pill-boxes. From their high level they were able to pour fire into some of the boats, ours among them.

Bullets struck men in the middle of our craft. The boat's ramp was lowered to let us get ashore, but the German fire caught those who tried to make it.

The remainder crouched inside, protected by armour and pouring return fire on the Nazis. Half a dozen men in field grey toppled from windows.

The Canadians fought a heroic battle from those craft still nosed up on the beach.

"MURDEROUS"

I lay behind a flimsy bit of armour-plating and heavy calibre bullets cut through it a couple of feet above my head.

An officer sitting next to me was firing a Sten gun. He killed at least one Nazi, and then was hit in the head. He fell forward bleeding profusely.

There were eight or ten in our boat who had been hit by now and a landing here seemed impossible.

The naval officer with us decided to get the boat off. We eased away from the shelling fire with nerve-racking slowness.

Off Dieppe, the raid flotilla remassed. Our wounded were sent to a hospital ship and I was transferred to another assault landing craft.

GUTTED BUILDINGS

Finally we got ashore for a few minutes right in front of the Dieppe esplanade. The smoke screen was so thick we could not see much and took off again. The area in front of the town, however, looked like a battleground with broken buildings gutted or burning in air sections.

By 10 a.m., Canadian troops, many of their actions led by tanks, had the town fairly well under control.

At noon, final re-embarkation of the troops was under way.

A demonstration of complete mastery of the sea and sky was given by the Navy and RAF. The Navy did a superlative job getting the large and complicated convoy to the right spots at the right time. They did it entirely without incident.

The dimensions of the air support defy adequate description.

▶ Troops unload supplies from a landing craft on to British soil after a raid on Dieppe.

LORD LOVAT LEADS CHARGE AT DIEPPE GUNS

By OUR SPECIAL CORRESPONDENT

WE landed west of Dieppe at dawn. The troops to whom I was attached, Lord Lovat's Number 4 Commando, were the first men of the raid force to jump ashore.

They had been told a few hours earlier by Admiral Lord Louis Mountbatten, Chief of Combined Operations, "Your task is most vital. If you don't knock out the German howitzer battery the whole operation will go wrong. You have got to do it even at the greatest possible risk."

They knew that if they failed, and the six German six-inch howitzers inland west of Dieppe bombarded the narrow Dieppe approach, there would be a great disaster.

They did not fail, and because of that, the Allied troops were able to land on their five appointed beaches.

We grounded on the shingle, a few yards from the foot of the hundred-foot chalk white cliffs.

As we blundered, bending, across the shingle to the cliff foot, a German machine-gun began to stutter from up above. Guns from our support craft answered. But for the moment we were under cover, brought in at the exact spot at the exactly appointed time (4.50 a.m.) by the Navy.

At the same moment the other half of 4 Commando, led by Lord Lovat himself, had landed a little further west. They were to try, by a wider dip in the cliffs, to take the battery in the rear while our force made the frontal attack.

We went up a crack in the cliff which ended in an almost vertical

beach staircase. Above that was a long gully.

In a few minutes the two banks of barbed wire at the top of the steps had been blasted with explosives, and the Commando spearhead, followed by a mortar platoon, were creeping cautiously up the gully.

Commando troopers were pleased with the air support.

Lord Louis Mountbatten had told them there would be two RAF fighters for every three men in the raid force, a proportion stronger than anything ever known since aerial warfare began.

ENGLISH WERE LAST TO LEAVE

From OUR SPECIAL CORRESPONDENT,
a South Coast Port, Thursday

EARLY today the last barge from Dieppe arrived in this harbour. The soldiers on board were all English.

Obviously fatigued, their uniforms soiled and tattered, they still formed up and marched out of the harbour towards the waiting transport as though they were coming off a parade ground.

"You would not think they had just come through one of the big battles of the war," an eye-witness said to me.

I have never seen anything so impressive as the unbroken discipline which took them through that raid and still made them march like the great soldiers they are.

A high Army officer who stood by to greet them was so moved that he jumped to attention and saluted them.

WOULDN'T TALK

The refusal of a British flight lieutenant who was shot down over Dieppe, to speak into a German microphone spoiled a German broadcast of the battle last night.

"Now we shall meet some prisoners – men from Canada and New Zealand and two British pilots who have been shot down," said the announcer.

"Hullo lieutenant," he went on in English. "You feel all right?"

"Yes, I feel all right," came a reply as from a distance.

"Won't you step a bit nearer and talk into the microphone?" said the German.

There was no reply and an awkward silence followed, which the Nazi tried in vain to cover up with another scene. – Reuter.

▶ German prisoners, captured in the raid on Dieppe in 1942, are blindfolded and escorted through the streets after the return of the commandos.

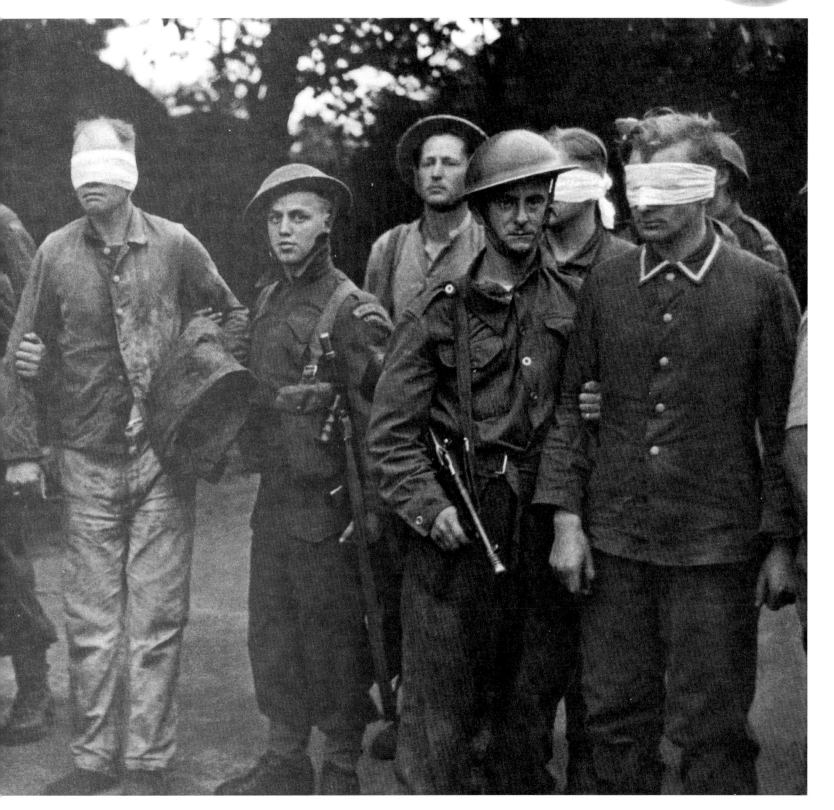

AFTERMATH OF DIEPPE RAID

This *Daily Mirror* picture was one of the first taken of German prisoners captured at Dieppe. They are blindfolded in the hands of their captors, but no more unseeing perhaps than they have been for years. Hitler told them they would come to England as conquerors – they came as captives, and will probably live longer for it. Many prisoners were taken in the raid and a Canadian officer expressed surprise that they were ready to give in so readily. Pictured are some of our Commandos on their return – one of whom left the leg of his trousers in Dieppe.

◗ Survivors of the Dieppe raid return to England.

AFTER THE RAID

"AN audacious experiment carried out with precision and bravado."
"We see in this adventure the shape of things to come."

Those quotations from the New York Press represent the first reaction to the news of the Dieppe raid. Hopes, inspiration are good things, after so many months of frustration. What about achievement?

The account of profit and loss has to be presented and analysed. The full facts have to be ascertained. After that we must expect a further reaction.

We must be prepared for heavy losses. And the question "was it worth while?" will sound in every argument.

It was worth while, surely, as a test, a feeler, and a valuable lesson. If we never attack we can never learn.

Were heavy losses avoidable? In what corners of the combined battlefield were mistakes made – mistakes that will not be described airily as bad luck? Questions like these must be answered with perfect frankness, without any attempt to deny or conceal the truth.

A RISK WORTH TAKING

Before the expert calculations are completed we can at least assert that the first political and psychological results are good and great. *We* have attacked. *They* have defended. The reversal of the usual process is, in itself, a tonic for the Allied cause. It has been so regarded, not only in America, but in Moscow, whence comes news of the great excitement roused by it.

If we remember this, we can ignore the Nazi propaganda which pronounces that the invasion which was not an invasion has been broken upon "impregnable defences." That Maginot-minded phrase resounds in Goebbels's whoops or wheedling

reassurances. We may admit that the German defences were strong. That, too, is something learnt by the experiment.

Meanwhile, after this biggest of our raids, we salute the men who have fulfilled our high expectations of their skill and valour in an adventure for which they have waited so long – prepared for the risk and willing to pay the price.

22 August **1942**

DIEPPE WOUNDED TELL THEIR STORY

NAZIS FIRED ON OUR MEN WHEN AIDING FALLEN

By A SPECIAL CORRESPONDENT

SURGEONS have been working day and night in Canadian military hospitals for the past forty-eight hours performing operations on the Dieppe raid wounded.

Emergency medical staffs were rushed to the hospitals as soon as the first boatload of survivors crossed the Channel.

Fleets of ambulances worked a shuttle service from the port of disembarkation and radiated, like spokes from a wheelhub, to the hospital bases in the south where hundreds of beds had been prepared.

In one Surrey hospital where British, Canadian and American soldiers were taken, operating teams – surgeons, anaesthetists, theatre sister and five nurses – have worked, night and day, never having taken their gowns and hoods off since the first ambulance arrived.

In one of the crowded wards I spoke to Sergeant Harry Roberts, of the Toronto Scottish, whose home is in Oakville, Ontario, and who had just come out of the anaesthetic after a bullet had been removed from his shoulder.

He grinned feebly as he showed me the memento.

"Jerry shot me in the back," he said. "I was bending down trying to lift my pal, who'd got it in the leg, when a Messerschmitt zoomed down and machine-gunned us."

"DIRTY" FIGHTERS

"He'd been as dirty as that all day. And when he wasn't dirty he was just plain heller-hi-yeller.

"It was pretty light when we landed on the beaches. I felt like letting out a whoop of a battlecry, but we'd been told to keep quiet.

"Not that it'd told Jerry any more than he knew because so soon as we stepped on to the beach he raked us murderously.

"When we got near to a pill-box full of Germans we let 'em have all that we'd got in our guns, but they were so yellow they'd neither fight nor come out.

"I climbed up on top of the concrete box and kicked the ventilator to bits. Then we threw hand grenades in and blew box and Jerries to blazes.

"There seemed far more Jerries about the place than I expected

to find. The few we got near we left deader'n if they'd never been born.

"When we'd done our job we began to return.

"When I got down to the beach, I saw our wounded had been brought there ready for the boats."

BULLET TO HIS WIFE

"Once the stretcher cases were on the boats, we had to follow. I waded out with half-a-dozen of my pals, but two of them were swept off their feet.

"I was half fainting with the pain from my shoulder where Jerry had got me and passed clean out in the ambulance once the excitement had passed. I'm sending the bullet off to my wife in Canada tomorrow, just to show her what her old man can put up with."

Since the ambulances brought the wounded to the Canadian hospitals, several of the men have died and others are not expected to live.

Hank Roberts wrote their epitaph when he said to me: "If it had gone the other way with me I'd have used my last breath to say it was worth it."

◀ Allied troops swap stories after returning from the raid on Dieppe. Canadian, British, American and a small contingent of French soldiers took part.

▶ Allied troops prepare to disembark after returning to England after the Dieppe raid.

24 August **1942**

DRAIN ON HUN PLANES

THERE is growing evidence that Germany is running short of planes. Deductions to this effect drawn from the way the German air operations were conducted over Dieppe last week are confirmed by statements made in Moscow on air fighting on the Russian front, states British United Press air correspondent.

At Dieppe, the most surprising feature was the late appearance of German fighters.

The operations had been in progress for some time before the German planes turned up. Evidence that the Germans had to go far and wide in Northern France and other occupied territories to get planes for the Dieppe fighting and bombing is considerable.

In spite of this the numbers they put into the air against us were not what might have been expected in such an all-out effort.

This is not to say that the numbers were not large: they were.

But there would have been no surprise this side of the Channel had they been much larger still.

The obvious explanation of any plane shortage on this side of Europe is that the German High Command is using the major part of its strength on the Eastern front, but a distinct shortage is apparent there, too.

27 August **1942**

"ADJUST THE MACHINE"

Now that the Prime Minister has returned to this country, after the most daring and dangerous of his war journeys, the nation is naturally anxious to hear what *immediate* practical results can be reasonably expected to follow from these vital conferences in Moscow and the Middle East.

Mr. Churchill has been "refreshed"—by his talks with Stalin and with General Smuts. What detailed plans have been made we must not expect to know. We do know that valiant determination must be backed by vigorous action *with all speed*. We know that time presses. We know that in Russia the military situation is grim. It was not "cheap sensationalism" that prompted the latest and gravest of Russian broadcasts on Monday night: that broadcast in which Yaroslavsky said – *we cannot afford to retreat any farther*.

AN ANXIOUS SITUATION

The situation was thus summarised by *The Times* yesterday:

The military situation which Mr. Churchill has found awaiting him on his return home is therefore certainly not less anxious than when he left these shores.

Neither the "dress rehearsal" of Dieppe nor the progressive bombing of the western nerve centres of the Nazi war production has relieved the continuing sense of an inadequacy in the British military achievement at a time when our Allies face a supreme crisis – a sense which translates itself in a demand not for premature or ill-considered action but for the strengthening of our military organisation and for its better adaptation to meet present emergencies.

28 August **1942**

ANOTHER CALL FOR SECOND FRONT

"The offensive spirit of the English and American peoples demands an issue," declared *Pravda* yesterday.

"Three years ago the men of Munich were called sages. Last year they were called fearful. Soon they will be called deserters.

"Every living man in Europe and America now demands an offensive. The honour of the world demands German blood."

16 September **1942**

DIEPPE – 3,350 LOST

The Canadian Department of National Defence announced yesterday that Canadian casualties at Dieppe totalled 3,350 killed, wounded and missing.

Forty officers and 130 other ranks were killed in action or had died of wounds, while forty-one officers and 592 men were wounded and 130 officers and 2,417 other ranks were missing.

18 September **1942**

His feet on the Nazi flag, is Ighty, mascot of a British motor-launch. He was the crew's only casualty in the Dieppe raid; he broke a leg by falling down a hatch during the action. The flag comes from the same raid. It was taken from a German armed tanker. The crew abandoned ship, and the M.L. men boarded and sank the tanker after taking the flag.

Back to the Drawing Board

The dead bodies that littered the beach at Dieppe served as a sobering influence on Allied plans to invade Europe. For most of the next two years military action was confined to naval battles in the Atlantic and infantry battles in North Africa, while Russia faced a furious assault from Hitler's army in the East. Talk of a second front became just that . . . talk. And there was a lot of it, at conferences in Casablanca, Quebec, Cairo and Tehran, where the "Big Three" of Churchill, Roosevelt and Stalin met for the first time.

◀ Winston Churchill and American President Franklin D. Roosevelt meet at Casablanca in January 1943, to lay down the unconditional surrender policy against the Axis Powers.

51

The conference at the Anfa Hotel in Casablanca includes (seated, left to right): Sir Charles Portal, Admiral Sir Dudley Pound, Winston Churchill (wearing the uniform of the Royal Air Force), Field Marshal Sir John Dill and General Sir Alan Brooke. Back row: General Sir Harold Alexander (third from left), Lord Louis Mountbatten (fifth from left), Major General Sir Hastings Ismay, Lord Leathers and Harold Macmillan (third from right).

A SAIL IN SIGHT

ROOSEVELT AND CHURCHILL IN NORTH AFRICA TEN-DAY TALK

MEET DE GAULLE AND GIRAUD

MR. CHURCHILL and President Roosevelt have met near Casablanca in North Africa, and, during ten days of non-stop conference, have planned a more intensive war drive in all spheres.

Stalin was invited, but could not attend because he is personally directing the Russian offensives.

De Gaulle and Giraud met at the conference and attended many of the talks.

By ARTHUR BROOKS

DAILY MIRROR SPECIAL CORRESPONDENT IN NORTH AFRICA

Casablanca, Tuesday

IN day and night talks extending to ten days, Mr. Churchill and President Roosevelt have – in collaboration with chiefs of staffs – surveyed the field of war theatre by theatre throughout the world, and marshalled all resources for more intense prosecution of the war by land, sea and air.

The conference is unprecedented in history, as it has taken in the whole world picture. Combined staffs have been in constant session, meeting two or three times a day and reporting progress at intervals to the President and Prime Minister.

General Alexander, British Commander-in-Chief, Middle East, and General Eisenhower, Allied Commander-in-Chief, North Africa, were present.

IT CAN BE CALLED THE UNCONDITIONAL SURRENDER CONFERENCE – THAT WAS PRESIDENT ROOSEVELT'S NAME FOR IT AT THE PRESS CONFERENCE

He indicated that peace could come to the world only by the total elimination of Axis war power which means unconditional surrender by Germany, Italy, Japan.

◀ As Churchill and Roosevelt discuss tactics in Casablanca, Stalin is leading Russian forces in the battle to defend Stalingrad from the Germans.

PREMIER IN U.S.

PUTTING FINAL TOUCHES TO SECOND FRONT PLAN

THE Prime Minister arrived in Washington last night to see President Roosevelt. He was accompanied by high military and naval advisers. Their conference is likely to be the most important one of the war.

The brief, dramatic announcement of Mr. Churchill's arrival was made at 1 a.m. today by Mr. Stephen Early, President Roosevelt's secretary. It said:

"Mr. Churchill has arrived in Washington. He was met by the President upon his arrival, and will be the President's guest for the duration of his visit. Mr. Churchill is accompanied by a staff of military and naval experts."

The announcement did not cast any light on the specific nature of Mr. Churchill's conversations with the President, and did not reveal the means by which he came.

A Columbia broadcast from Washington said that Lord Beaverbrook had also arrived in Washington. "Other members of the British party have not yet been announced," the commentator added.

The new talks between Churchill and Roosevelt are expected to go far beyond plans for landing Allied troops on the Continent, John Walters, *Daily Mirror* New York correspondent, cabled early today.

A tremendous development in the war is expected as soon as the result of the talks is known. The trend of these developments will surprise the world, according to reliable observers.

One said: "The coming events will astonish and disconcert the Axis. Churchill and Roosevelt are out-matching past record of Hitler for bold moves."

Premier and President are meeting to discuss the next step in the final phase of the defeat of Germany. That much is admitted, writes the *Daily Mirror* Diplomatic Correspondent.

In London it is understood that the main items to be considered are:

Final details for the opening of a European Front.
The provision of the necessary shipping.
Distribution of armaments and men as between the Far Eastern and the European fronts.
Selection of commanders.

More elaborate precautions were taken to guard the secrecy of Mr. Churchill's departure than on any of his previous trips from this country. The Premier motored to a suburban station, where he joined his special train.

◀ Winston Churchill gives the V sign to sailors as he disembarks his ship upon arrival in America for talks with President Roosevelt.

20 May 1943

PREMIER'S TRIUMPH PROMISES U.S. FULL HELP IN BRINGING JAPAN TO ASHES

F.D.R. MAY MEET STALIN

U-BOAT IS WORST MENACE

MR. CHURCHILL scored one of his greatest personal triumphs when he spoke to the world from the United States Congress in Washington last night.

When he appeared in the House of Representatives a roar of cheering and shouting went up that lasted for three minutes, and his speech was constantly interrupted by roars of applause.

Many Congressmen said the speech was the greatest of his career.

Early on he delighted his listeners by his assurance that "we British have at least as great an interest as the United States in the unflinching and relentless waging of war against Japan."

This remark was greeted with cheers, for there has been an unhappy and unwarranted feeling in America – fostered by Isolationists and those who hate Roosevelt – that England was interested only in the war against Germany, and, that won, would leave America to fight Japan.

"I am here to tell you," continued Mr. Churchill, "that we will wage that war side by side with you while there is breath in our bodies and while blood flows through our veins . . ."

EVERY MAN AND GUN

"I repudiate the slightest suspicions that we should hold back anything that could be usefully employed, or that I and the Government I represent are not resolved to employ every man, gun and aeroplane that can be used in this business." Mr. Churchill referred to the necessity of laying the cities of Japan in ashes, "for in ashes they must lie before peace comes back to the world."

At this the applause broke out in waves again.

SOVIET OFFENSIVE HAS BEGUN, SAYS BERLIN

THE great Soviet offensive, which has been expected for several days, has begun, according to Berlin radio.

It started with fierce attacks on the Kuban bridgehead on the Donetz, supported by planes and tanks, Berlin added. It was claimed that the attacks had been thrown back with a loss of fifteen tanks.

The German statement is the first hint of the ending of the lull on the Russian front: last night's Soviet communiqué did not mention any such attacks.

2 November 1943

VICTORY PLANS IN WHAT COMMENTATORS DESCRIBE AS THE MAGNA CHARTA OF MODERN TIMES, THE FOREIGN SECRETARIES OF BRITAIN, RUSSIA AND AMERICA DREW UP AT THE MOSCOW CONFERENCE THIS PLAN, OUTLINED IN A COMMUNIQUÉ

ISSUED FROM DOWNING-STREET LAST NIGHT: GERMANS concerned in atrocities and executions are to be taken back to the countries where the crimes were committed and tried under those countries' laws.

MEASURES to shorten the war in Europe were thrashed out in frank and exhaustive discussions.

UNCONDITIONAL surrender remains the Allies' aim.

CLOSER collaboration between the three countries and China, and inclusion of all peace-loving nations in a system of international co-operation.

AUSTRIA'S independence is to be restored.

AN advisory commission is to be established to deal with questions affecting Europe.

Winston Churchill (centre) marks his 69th birthday with a party at the British Embassy in Tehran on 30 November 1943. Among the guests were President Roosevelt (left) and Marshal Stalin. Stalin proposed a toast to "my fighting friend, Churchill", and Churchill raised a glass to "Stalin the Great" and "Roosevelt the man".

STALIN HAS BEEN GIVEN OUR PLANS

By OUR POLITICAL CORRESPONDENT

OF first importance in the communiqué is the paragraph about future military operations.

These discussions referred to what Moscow has always termed the "Second Front." It is understood that Marshal Stalin is in possession of all our plans.

It was on this point that close observers most feared difficulties but the announcement that there will be "the closest military co-operation" makes it clear that agreement was reached.

The decision to carry into peace the close co-operation and collaboration begun during war is the most shrewd blow yet struck at German propaganda.

Nazi leaders have been laying plans by which, if they lost the war in a military sense, they would deal only with Britain and America in making peace and the resettlement of Europe.

THE BIGGEST THING EVER IS COMING – SMUTS

GENERAL SMUTS, the Empire's senior statesman, declared in a dramatic speech yesterday that "the greatest thing that ever happened inside a century or in centuries" is coming.

"Everything is in order and is moving towards that great conclusion," he said. "I hope this will be the last Christmas of the war. By next Christmas I hope we will be going home with victory in our pockets."

General Smuts, lifelong friend of Churchill and a member of the War Cabinet for the duration of his recent visit to London, was addressing a Press conference in Cairo, where he called, on his way home from Britain, to see Mr. Churchill and President Roosevelt.

The General said: "I am returning to South Africa more confident and more convinced of victory than ever before.

"The most critical situation has been in the diplomatic fields in which at least three of the greatest Powers of the world have been engaged with the possibility that one or another of them would not see eye to eye with the others."

BURIED IN WESTERN DESERT

"We are now absolutely undivided for final victory. Next year will probably be one of the most decisive years in human history.

"The old order into which I was born lies buried in the Western Desert."

Marshal Voroshilov shows a special sword, presented to Stalin by Churchill to mark the Russian victory at the Battle of Stalingrad, to President Roosevelt, while Churchill and Stalin look on.

D-Day

When Clementine Churchill went to bed on the evening of 5 June 1944, her husband Winston said to her: "By the time you wake up in the morning, 20,000 young men may have been killed." And Field-Marshal Lord Alanbrooke, the Chief of the Imperial General Staff, wrote in his diary on 5 June: "I am very uneasy about the whole operation." Operation Overlord began just before dawn on 6 June. By the evening more than 150,000 Allied troops were safely ashore. Despite Churchill's fears, the death toll was 4,500. Finally, a second front was a reality.

◆ Part of the British invasion fleet bound for the Gold, Juno and Sword Normandy beaches are seen here on the morning of D-Day from the cliffs overlooking Folkestone. Royal Navy destroyers lay a smokescreen to hide the fleet from the French coast.

61

"S-S-Stop s-s-saying 'S-S-Say W-When'!"

2 June **1944**

"OUR HOUR OF ACTION IS AT HAND"

Mr. Stimson, U.S. Secretary for War, declared yesterday: "The period of decisive action is at hand."

Movement of U.S. troops to the combat areas is rapidly nearing the peak, he told a Press conference.

The U.S. Army has 3,657,000 soldiers deployed throughout the world "striking and preparing to strike victory winning blows by land, sea and air against Germany and Japan."

Declaring that the Royal Navy will have a great part to play in our invasion, Admiral Sir William M. James, Chief of Naval Information at the Admiralty, said in London yesterday: "We shall have dramatic moments soon. Before long, we shall reach that stage when we begin to launch a great amphibious expedition."

UNDER 18S CALLED

Men born between July 1, 1926, and September 30, 1926, inclusive, must register for National Service tomorrow. Those who have already registered must do so again.

◀ Philip Zec's cartoon, published on 21 April 1944, shows 6 June as a possible invasion date. Many *Daily Mirror* readers wrote to the paper after D-Day to ask how he knew.

5 June **1944**

INVASION FLASH BY JOAN SET U.S. ABLAZE

From JOHN SAMPSON,
New York, Sunday

ENGLISH teletype-operator and former Waaf, 22-year-old Joan Ellis, became the most talked about woman in America today – and all because she made a slip.

On Saturday afternoon long awaited news flashed into newspaper offices. It electrified America. Radio programmes were interrupted for it, men, women and children danced in the streets, the White House was deluged with telephone calls, churches were filled with worshipping throngs.

And all because Joan, sitting practising at her teletype machine in the London office of Associated Press, had punched out on her disconnected machine: "Flash, London, Eisenhower's Headquarters announces Allied landings in France."

At this moment came the real communiqué. Joan turned on her machine and the perforated tape, bearing the vital flash, ran through the machine before anyone noticed it.

Within two minutes, editors had caught the error.

No papers with the news got on to the street, but N.B.C. interrupted its radio broadcast – and one station put a commentator on with prepared copy to describe how troops were fighting

Today, with life back to normal, Americans are asking, "What's going to happen to Joan Ellis?"

6 June **1944**

FRENCH COAST GETS IT AGAIN

THE French "invasion coast" and key points in Northern France and Belgium got another full-scale blasting from the air yesterday.

Highlight of the attacks was another onslaught on the Boulogne and Calais area by massed Forts and Liberators. From 500 to 750 of the heavies were out, with an escort of 500 fighters.

The mighty campaign to paralyse Nazi communications was carried on by fighter-bombers and rocket-carrying Typhoons. More bridges were hit, and seventeen locomotives destroyed in Northern France and Belgium. Factories were also hit.

Rocket and bomb-carrying RAF Typhoons made successful attacks on eight more Nazi radio installations along the northern coast of France and in the Channel Isles.

Two of the targets were each subjected to two powerful attacks and extensive damage was seen. There was no fighter opposition, but extremely heavy flak was encountered at some points.

Flak stations which tried to beat off our bombers were dive-bombed by Thunderbolt fighters.

"BACK FOR PETROL" RAID

Paris radio said that the region of the capital was one of our targets.

Mustangs adopted a new technique yesterday.

Returning from escorting Fortresses and Liberators, they spotted a German military convoy, hurried home, refuelled, bombed up, and flashed back again across the Channel to unleash a load of high explosives on their unsuspecting prey.

Great activity by heavy RAF planes began unusually early last night, and from 9.15 onwards planes were heard roaring out in great strength over the East Coast. Later German radio said planes were approaching Western Germany.

Daily Mirror

JUNE 7

No. 12,627
ONE PENNY
Registered
at the G.P.O.
as
a Newspaper.

✦ ✦ ✦

4,000 ships and 11,000 planes take part in attack

German shore guns are quelled—Churchill

WE HOLD BEACHHEAD

Bristol 0 50 Miles. Chatham Dover Calais Dunkirk Southampton Portsmouth Newhaven Boulogne Weymouth R. Somme Abbeville Amiens Cherbourg Dieppe Barfleur Havre Trouville Rouen R. Seine Guernsey Jersey Caen R. Orne Versailles PARIS Chartres

WITHIN a few hours of the mightiest assault in history Allied troops established a beachhead on the Normandy coast yesterday.

Airborne troops are fighting some miles inland. More than 640 naval guns—from 4 to 16 inches—had practically silenced the German coastal batteries. The Allied air force was in absolute control.

All through the day, from the 7 a.m. landings until dusk, Allied fighter-bombers were dive-bombing, glide-bombing and strafing German defences and communications. They flew into the mouths of guns and dived within feet of the bridges.

EISENHOWER HAD 11,000 PLANES FOR THE JOB, AND HIS EXPERTS FORESAW 20,000 SORTIES IN THE DAY.

Scaled the Cliffs

Berlin provided the only place-names in the news. They said they were fighting Allied troops on an eighty-mile front between Trouville and Barfleur, on the Cherbourg peninsula.

They spoke of hard fighting around Caen, and of landings in the Seine Bay area.

Tanks, they said, were landed at Aromanches, fifteen miles from Caen, nine hours after the main landings.

In this landing there were 200 boats, and Berlin spoke of:

"THE ENEMY TRYING TO SCALE THE STEEP COAST WITH THE AID OF SPECIAL LADDERS."

Other landings were being made under strong air protection at Ouistreham and Marcoeuf, and Berlin added: "the landing parties were at once engaged in extremely costly battles."

There is no word at all from the Allied side to support the German statement that we have landed paratroops on Guernsey and Jersey, which lie off the coast.

Hitler's biggest admission was that between Caen and Isigny the Allied tanks had penetrated several miles to the south.

"What a Plan!"

Mr. Churchill gave the House the facts at noon. "This is the first of a series of landings," he emphasised.

BEFORE SUNRISE YESTERDAY AN ARMADA OF 4,000 SHIPS, WITH SEVERAL THOUSAND SMALLER CRAFT, HAD CROSSED THE CHANNEL—WHICH WAS NOT TOO KIND AND SMOOTH.

Mass airborne landings had been successfully effected. The fire of the shore batteries had been largely quelled and landing on the beaches was proceeding.

THE ANGLO - AMERICAN ALLIES ARE
(Continued on Back Page)

20,000 SORTIES

●

CHANNEL ISLAND ATTACK

—German Report

What the Huns said

The German radio made the first announcement to the world yesterday morning, and throughout the day their military commentators and experts never stopped talking.

"They are coming, they are coming," shouted Captain Sertorius, and Lieutenant-Colonel von Olberg, more dignified, said: "D-Day has dawned—the invasion has begun. There is every indication that the present Allied intention is a triphibious offensive which MUST BE TAKEN VERY SERIOUSLY INDEED."

The enemy radio said the invasion began with the landing of airborne troops near the mouth of the Seine, and asserted that the operations extended from Le Havre to Caen to Cherbourg.

Their early reports said that

"First British prisoner"

Private James Griffith, of Newcastle, was one of the first prisoners to be captured by the Germans, said German radio. He had been fighting in the Caen and Cherbourg region. "The fighting was tough," he said.

German naval forces were in action off the coast, and later claimed that a large Allied warship had been set on fire off the Seine where many Allied ships were gathered.

The Allied fleet was then given as six heavy warships and twenty destroyers.

Le Havre harbour was being bombarded, the Germans announced, and Anglo-American paratroops "baled out on the northern tip of Normandy to capture several airfields."

As the day went the German admissions increased.

Airborne landings were made "in great depth"—and shortly after this was altered to "greater depth."

Allied troops, they said, were fighting ten miles inland from the coast.

"At least four U.S.A. and British parachute and airborne divisions were in action between Le Havre and Cherbourg."

German air defence forces attacked, it was claimed, and a further statement insisted that "many sections of parachute units have been wiped out." Another report, not quite so certain, said that they were only "badly mauled."

The Germans admitted that the Anglo-American troops fighting at the mouth of the Seine had been reinforced but added hopefully:—

"Strong winds and rain showers are harassing the enemy units laden with tanks and troops, in particular the smaller ones. They are trying to evade the withering fire of

Continued on Back Page

Barfleur, fifteen miles east of Cherbourg, is the start of a great road and rail triangle, leading into a rocky plain.

The Isle of Wight can be seen on a clear day, seventy miles away. The sea, hereabouts, is rock strewn and dangerous.

"FIGHTING ALONG 80 MILES"

●

Sky troops sweep in

●

MINEFIELD HAZARDS OVERCOME

➡ Canadian troops wade ashore in Normandy on D-Day.

ROOSEVELT

IT IS suggested that Mr. Roosevelt contemplates a visit to these islands. We hope the report is true. No visitor could be more welcome at the present juncture – both on personal and political grounds – than the President of the United States, whose position in world affairs stands high today. There are grave matters to be dealt with on this side of the Atlantic.

The future political settlement, no less than the immediate liberation of Europe, is the supreme task of the hour; a problem which will tax the brains, the energies, and the patience of all concerned. So far no really firm foundation of Allied co-operation has been established . . .

MOVIES WANT HER

Mary Churchill [the youngest of Winston Churchill's five children, aged 21 at the time] has been offered a post-war Hollywood movie contract, says a New York newspaper.

7 June **1944**

WE HOLD BEACHHEAD

WITHIN a few hours of the mightiest assault in history Allied troops established a beachhead on the Normandy coast yesterday.

Airborne troops are fighting some miles inland. More than 640 naval guns – from 4 to 16 inches – had practically silenced the

German coastal batteries. The Allied air force was in absolute control.

All through the day, from the 7 a.m. landings until dusk, Allied fighter-bombers were dive-bombing, glide-bombing and strafing German defences and communications. They flew into the mouths of guns and dived within feet of the bridges.

EISENHOWER HAD 11,000 PLANES FOR THE JOB, AND HIS EXPERTS FORESAW 20,000 SORTIES IN THE DAY.

SCALED THE CLIFFS

Berlin provided the only place-names in the news. They said they were fighting Allied troops on an eighty-mile front between Trouville and Barfleur, on the Cherbourg peninsula.

They spoke of hard fighting around Caen, and of landings in the Seine Bay area.

Tanks, they said, were landed at Arromanches, fifteen miles from Caen, nine hours after the main landings.

In this landing there were 200 boats, and Berlin spoke of:

"THE ENEMY TRYING TO SCALE THE STEEP COAST WITH THE AID OF SPECIAL LADDERS."

Other landings were being made under strong air protection at Ouistreham and Marcoeuf, and Berlin added: "the landing parties were at once engaged in extremely costly battles."

There is no word at all from the Allied side to support the German statement that we have landed paratroops on Guernsey and Jersey, which lie off the coast.

Hitler's biggest admission was that between Caen and Isigny the Allied tanks had penetrated several miles to the south.

"WHAT A PLAN!"

Mr. Churchill gave the House the facts at noon. "This is the first of a series of landings," he emphasised.

BEFORE SUNRISE YESTERDAY AN ARMADA OF 4,000 SHIPS, WITH SEVERAL THOUSAND SMALLER CRAFT, HAD CROSSED THE CHANNEL – WHICH WAS NOT TOO KIND AND SMOOTH.

Mass airborne landings had been successfully effected. The fire of the shore batteries had been largely quelled and landing on the beaches was proceeding.

"THE ANGLO-AMERICAN ALLIES ARE SUSTAINED BY ABOUT 11,000 FIRST LINE AIRCRAFT," SAID THE PRIME MINISTER.

"So far," he went on, "the commanders who are engaged, report that everything is proceeding according to plan – and what a plan!

"THERE ARE ALREADY HOPES THAT ACTUAL TACTICAL SURPRISE HAS BEEN ATTAINED AND

WE HOPE TO FURNISH THE ENEMY WITH A SUCCESSION OF SURPRISES DURING THE COURSE OF THE FIGHTING.

"The battle which has now begun will grow constantly in scale and intensity for many weeks to come, and I shall not attempt to speculate on its course, but this I may say: Complete unity prevails."

Assembly areas for the great enterprise started to get ready on Sunday. Strangely, the Germans do not seem to have realised the imminence of the invasion, and they did very little interference.

Bomber Command kept up the intensity of its battering of the French coast all day on Monday, and then at 11.30 p.m. it loosed its invasion force, 1,300 planes, which raked the landing zones from midnight to sunrise.

AFTER THEM CAME THE NAVY, WITH 10,000 MEN, ON THE BIGGEST MINE-SWEEPING JOB IN HISTORY.

LITTLE OPPOSITION

Berlin radio said "the sky was darkened by the enormous swarm of Allied planes, which came over in enormous waves."

Correspondents say that General Montgomery is in actual charge of the operation. General Eisenhower stood on a rooftop and watched them go.

British, U.S. and Canadian Forces are engaged, but Frenchmen are not being used until later.

The first Allied infantry scrambled ashore at 7 a.m., in two areas, apparently without heavy opposition.

Huge fleets of Allied warships covered the landing with supporting bombardment according to fighter pilots, and Flying Fortresses were bombing the beach.

One of the picturesque stories of the day came from Lieutenant-Colonel C.A. Shoop, when he flew back from France.

"We have established some good beachheads and are slashing our way inland," he said.

He expressed surprise at the lack of opposition to our air, ground and naval forces.

"There are lots of burning buildings and bomb craters," he went on. "Towns are burning all over the area."

He was impressed with the speed of the landing operations. "Everything seemed to be moving very fast," he commented. "I saw many of our troops running."

As the paratroops descended they shouted, "Here we come, Hitler."

American forces drive up on to the beach in an amphibian vehicle from their landing craft.

American forces prepare to come ashore in Normandy on D-Day.

British and Allied troops on the beaches of Normandy after the
D-Day landings.

THEIR RATIONS

Each man of the invading army was issued with one day's emergency rations for the first day's operations; after that field kitchens will be in operation. The landing vessels had eight days' rations aboard.

WHAT THE HUNS SAID

The German radio made the first announcement to the world yesterday morning, and throughout the day their military commentators and experts never stopped talking.

"They are coming, they are coming," shouted Captain Sertorius, and Lieutenant-Colonel von Olberg, more dignified, said: "D-Day has dawned – the invasion has begun. There is every indication that the present Allied intention is a triphibious offensive which MUST BE TAKEN VERY SERIOUSLY INDEED."

The enemy radio said the invasion began with the landing of airborne troops near the mouth of the Seine, and asserted that the operations extended from Le Havre to Caen to Cherbourg.

As the day went the German admissions increased.

Airborne landings were made "in great depth" – and shortly after this was altered to "greater depth."

Allied troops, they said, were fighting ten miles inland from the coast.

"At least four U.S.A. and British parachute and airborne divisions were in action between Le Havre and Cherbourg."

German air defence forces attacked, it was claimed, and a further statement insisted that "many sections of parachute units have been wiped out." Another report, not quite so certain, said that they were only "badly mauled."

▶ Infantry carry their bicycles ashore from a landing craft.

ALLIED LEADERS' "FREEDOM COMING" BATTLE-CRY TO WAITING EUROPE

DRAMATIC to the highest degree was the manner in which the people of Europe were told that the hour they had been waiting for had struck – that the invasion had actually begun. Yet there was no fanfare – just grim, tense realism.

B.B.C. announcers read the first communiqué recording the landing then called on all the people of Western Europe to muster at their radios to hear a vital announcement by General Eisenhower from Supreme H.Q., Allied Expeditionary Force.

◀ Streams of American troops come ashore in Normandy.

The Allied C.-in-C. calmly but impressively issued his instructions to them but there was no mistaking the momentous and historic nature of the occasion.

He was followed at the radio by King Haakon, of Norway, Professor P. S. Gerbrandy, Prime Minister of the Netherlands, M. Hubert Pierlot, Prime Minister of Belgium. The accumulative effect of these broadcasts achieved the very peak of solemnity.

"LIBERATION SOON" – EISENHOWER

Broadcasting to Western Europe and the people of France, General Eisenhower said:

PEOPLE OF WESTERN EUROPE, A LANDING was made this morning on the coast of France by troops of the Allied Expeditionary Force.

This landing is part of the concerted United Nations' plan for the liberation of Europe, made in conjunction with our great Russian Allies. I have this message for all of you. Although the initial assault may not have been made in your own country the hour of your liberation is approaching.

All patriots, men and women, young and old, have a part to play in the achievement of final victory.

To members of resistance movements, whether led by nationals or by outside leaders, I say "Follow the instructions you have received."

To patriots who are not members of organised resistance groups I say "Continue your passive resistance, but do not needlessly endanger your lives. Wait until I give you the signal to rise and strike the enemy. The day will come when I shall need your united strength."

TO THE CITIZENS OF FRANCE

I AM proud to have again under my command the gallant forces of France. Fighting beside their Allies they will play a worthy part in the liberation of their homeland.

Follow the instructions of your leaders. A premature uprising of all Frenchmen may prevent you from being of maximum help to your country in the critical hour. Be patient. Prepare.

The effective civil administration of France must be provided by Frenchmen. All persons must continue in their present duties, unless otherwise instructed.

Those who have made common cause with the enemy and so betrayed their country will be removed.

When France is liberated from her oppressors you, yourselves, will choose your representatives and a Government under which you wish to live.

This landing is but the opening phase of the campaign in Western Europe. Great battles lie ahead. I call upon all who love freedom to stand with us. Keep your faith staunch. Our arms are resolute. Together we shall achieve victory.

FIRST BRITISH PRISONER

Private James Griffith, of Newcastle, was one of the first prisoners to be captured by the Germans, said German radio. He had been fighting in the Caen and Cherbourg region.

"The fighting was tough," he said.

SEVEN LONE INVADERS WERE THE 'KEY MEN'

From IAN FYFE, Your Correspondent
with an Airborne Unit

SEVEN men of this airborne unit early yesterday vied for an honour that will make their names household words.

It was a strange and grim competition, for the men – all officers – were the first Allied soldiers to land in Europe. Each officer wanted to be the first man to touch down in France. They jumped by parachute, leading in volunteer squads of airborne pathfinders.

On landing in enemy territory a short time before H hour, D day – literally a matter of minutes before the invasion started – they prepared landing grounds for battalions of paratroopers and airborne infantry in gliders.

Their job was a key one – and one of the most hazardous in the operation. It had been a "best-kept" secret.

The officers who led the "pathfinders" are Major F.G.L. Lennox-Boyd, of Henlow, Beds; Captain I.A. Tait, West Meon, Hants; Lieutenant M. Moore, Lake District; Lieutenant de Latour, London, S.W.; Lieutenant D. Wells, London, S.W.; Lieutenant R. Midwood, Scarborough; Lieutenant J. Vischer, Newport Pagnell, Bucks.

The men themselves had been laying side-bets on which officer would wear the first Allied boots to touch down on enemy territory.

One of the officers told me: "Yes, we have what most people would call a tough job, but we will do it.

"It is going to be interesting to see who gets the honour of being the first one to land."

KEEN AS MUSTARD

"The men are in magnificent trim and as keen as mustard. There is no doubt they will fight and work hard to do the job they are sent in to do.

"They realise what depends on it, and we have complete faith in them as they have confidence in us."

Like everyone else in this vast operation every one of the "pathfinders" was trained to the last and most minute detail.

They had a wide picture of the entire operation – and they know just what to do and when to do it.

⬥ British troops capture German prisoners but come under fire on Juno beach shortly after the D-Day landings.

GREAT ARMADA STRETCHED OVER HORIZON

JOHN HOGAN, your own correspondent with the Merchant Navy, yesterday cabled this picture of the immense convoy fleet on the eve of the historic D-Day

THE guns have been finally checked, and the ships' clocks on board synchronised. Everything is now ready for the signal to hoist anchor and sail with our cargo of men, ammunition, petrol and mines.

Months of preparations have ended. Invasion talk, gossip and speculation are no more. Zero hour has come.

For twenty-four hours we have known we shall sail soon.

Imagine the biggest lake you know plastered with bobbing autumn leaves and you have a picture of what I can see from the salt-sprayed bridge of our ship.

Everywhere on the sea are steel ships. You can't get away from them, can't look anywhere without seeing long lines of troopships, supply vessels, assault craft and warships – stretching away to faint blobs on the horizon.

Hundreds of ships ride at anchor in our convoy. Big ones that carried passengers, small ones that used to be grimed with coal dust, and strange ones that will race to the beachheads loaded with Commandos, tanks and bulldozers.

I sailed for hours, and still had miles to go before the leading vessel of this gigantic convoy came up within sight.

Today has been just another day on board this coaster, if you overlook the dozens of soldiers who swarm over the decks and live in a huge canvas tent slung on deck.

Brown tents are to be seen everywhere. Sleek warships are alongside us, and minesweepers stretch out on the port side.

The waiting seamen and soldiers have turned the ship into a fun fair.

John Fuller, of Anlaby Road, Hull, a big husky seaman of 20, has skippered a comic football team on the battened forward hold.

I asked Fuller, the Tommy Trinder of the crew, how he felt about setting sail in a couple of hours.

"Me? Bloody champion, I feel. I can't get there soon enough."

For Jack Upperton, of South View road, Southwick, Essex, the invasion will satisfy a curiosity born off the beaches of Dunkirk when he brought back 1,560 men, and was machine-gunned by German E-boats.

Nearly all the men have shaved.

"Damn it, we must make ourselves presentable when we call on Jerry," explained one.

Four years ago, Sergeant Harry Campbell, of Arrochar, Dumbarton, left France.

"The French people smiled," he said, "and told me, 'You'll be back.' I didn't think I would, but here I am, all set and busting anxious to get back on the Continent."

DESTINY'S HOUR

THE hour of destiny for Europe, and perhaps for the whole of mankind, has struck. A simple announcement, followed by the

The Hour of Reckoning. (June 7, 1944)

homely tones of General Eisenhower on the radio, proclaimed a world-shaking event, the like of which has no parallel in history. What began in Northern France yesterday morning marks the final phase in the greatest war of all time, and is the largest, most elaborate, most intrepid operation of its kind ever undertaken. Our

first thoughts in this solemn hour must be with the men of the Allied Armies who have landed with our banners – the banners of Hope and Freedom – and are determined, despite all dangers and difficulties, to carry them across Europe and in due course to plant them in the heart of Berlin. Some of these men have fought in many lands and have won much glory. Others are newer to the bloody game of war, but are of great heart. The task before them may be stupendous, but they will perform it stupendously. It is impossible to say how long this final phase of the struggle will last. Possibly, it will reach its inevitable end quicker than some people suppose. While there is, at present, every sign that the enemy will fight with skill and desperate energy, there remains the one great imponderable factor of how the German people react to a war which is inexorably drawing closer and closer to German soil. Meantime there are hard days to endure.

On a memorable occasion, and at a time when there seemed little left to us except hope and that sublime obstinacy which is the British character expressed in terms of adversity, the Prime Minister, with inspiring pessimism, promised us blood, tears and sweat. It is blood, tears and sweat that we face again today, but in a very different mood. Then the skies were grey. Now they are ablaze with the light of triumphs achieved, and victory to come. On behalf of those who have gone forth in courage and cheerful fortitude to fight this epic battle we, at home, offer our prayers, and pledge ourselves to support them in mind, in spirit, in material, to the utmost of our capacity.

The curtain rises on the closing scene of the greatest human conflict the world has ever known. To many people this is a holy war because it represents the eternal struggle between Good and Evil. As our hearts swell with pride and awe; as we contemplate the perils and glories of the battle; as we offer up our humble supplication; we can, with reason, select a sacred invocation for the battle cry, and say, with Montgomery: "Let God arise, and let His enemies be scattered."

⬥ Allied troops and piles of ammunition boxes and supplies stand on the Normandy invasion beaches.

EISENHOWER'S MESSAGE TO EVERY SOLDIER

General Dwight D. Eisenhower's Order of the Day, distributed to every man of the assault forces yesterday after he embarked, and read by Commanders to all other troops in the Allied Expeditionary Force, said:

SOLDIERS, SAILORS AND AIRMEN OF THE ALLIED EXPEDITIONARY FORCE:

You are about to embark upon the great crusade towards which we have striven these many months.

The eyes of the world are upon you. The hopes and prayers of liberty-loving people everywhere march with you.

In company with our brave allies and brothers-in-arms on other fronts you will bring about the destruction of the German war machine, the elimination of Nazi tyranny over the oppressed peoples of Europe, and security for ourselves in a free world.

Your task will not be an easy one. Your enemy is well trained, well-equipped and battle-hardened. He will fight savagely.

But this is the year 1944! Much has happened since the Nazi triumphs of 1940–41. The United Nations have inflicted upon the Germans great defeats in open battle, man to man.

Our air offensive has seriously reduced their strength in the air, and their capacity to wage war on the ground.

Our home fronts have given us an overwhelming superiority in weapons and munitions of war, and placed at our disposal great reserves of trained fighting men. The tide has turned! The free men of the world are marching together to victory!

I have full confidence in your courage, devotion to duty and skill in battle. We will accept nothing less than full victory!

Good luck! And let us all beseech the blessing of Almighty God upon this great and noble undertaking.

➤ American soldiers give artificial respiration to a colleague who nearly drowned during the beach landing.

➤ Philip Zec's cartoon in the *Daily Mirror* of 8 June 1944 captures the reality of the Allied landings in Normandy.

There's a long, long trail a-winding . . .

ALLIED CHIEFS MEET AT SEA, PLAN BATTLE

General Eisenhower, with Admiral Ramsay, cruised off the invasion beaches and held a series of conferences with his operational commanders for four and a half hours yesterday afternoon.

General Montgomery, Admiral Kirk, field commanders whose names are still secret, and commanders of the task forces which launched the invasion, conferred with the C.-in-C. This audacious trip was made in an unescorted British warship, which at one point took him only five miles from the enemy.

HUNS HOPE TO DRIVE WEDGES

From GEORGE McCARTHY,
Daily Mirror Chief Correspondent, Allied Advanced Command,
Wednesday night

WITH the landing beaches cleared of the enemy, the battle has moved inland, and the Germans are fighting hard.

They hope to drive deep wedges in the Allied line, cut the invasion troops into fragments – and drive them out.

So far this plan has had no success. Every counter-attack has been beaten off. In the fighting last night an enemy battalion headquarters was captured.

But the German resistance is stiffening as his reserves come into action.

Heavy movements of German troops have been seen on all the roads leading north to the assault bay.

It is known that the heavy blows inflicted by our bombing have slowed his move. . . .

HOW WE DID IT – TOLD BY SOME OF THE MEN WHO WERE FIRST ASHORE

THIS is the story of how our men stormed their way on to the shores of Hitler's Europe – told by some of the men who did it.

It is a story that adds to the honours of a famous North Country Division and the first narrator is Sergeant George Maynard of Yorkshire, who was hit by a grenade as he fought his way up through a wood and has arrived back in Britain.

HOW WE GOT THERE

Troops are wading through the surf to the shore from landing craft. The beaches are alive with men, equipment and vehicles, and there is more to follow. Smoke is clouding the skyline, because the Allied warships out in the Channel are putting over a hail of shells.

The invasion craft is now a mercy ... ore. Orderlies care for the wounded.

... nd stretcher cases are carefully for transport to hospitals.

Our nurses are over there, too

By Your Special Correspondent

NURSES are already in the invasion battle area tending the wounded as they are brought in by stretcher bearers from the front line.

They are working at casualty clearing stations in forward areas, as well as at base hospitals which have been set up in the coastal strip of reconquered territory.

Wounded men are being sent back to Britain as soon as they can be shipped or sent by air. A fleet of air ambulances is working a ferry service. Nurses are with the men on their way across the Channel.

In this country the wounded will be dispersed to military and civilian emergency hospitals in all parts of the country. Most of them will be in "safe" and "non-target" areas.

News for Relatives

Next of kin will be informed that their men have been wounded directly the news reaches the War Office.

In most cases this will be before the men arrive in Britain. Special reinforcements of nursing and medical personnel, together with all the latest surgical equipment, have been installed in several South Coast hospitals.

After about sixty wounded British soldiers had been landed from an L.S.T. craft, at a south of England port, a correspondent talked to a staff officer. His opinion was that casualties were very light so far.

It was significant, he thought, that the craft, which carried its own operating theatre and comfortably housed 400 wounded, had brought back only about sixty.

A correspondent describing the landing scenes from the Canadian ship Prince David says the first casualties he saw were men of the Royal Marine Commandos.

Casualties arriving yesterday in a hospital train from a southern port were met by doctors and nurses and taken in a fleet of ambulances to a hospital in the Home Counties.

Within a short time of their arrival they were receiving attention from a medical staff which specialises in plastic surgery.

The men's arrival had been kept secret. The arrival of ambulances outside the station, however, indicated something unusual, and the news spread quickly.

People waved as the ambulances sped by, and shouted words of encouragement.

Nearly all taxis at a north-west town were commandeered last night as emergency ambulances.

Another wounded British soldier being carried ashore.

81

He said: "We landed soon after seven a.m. from an assault craft. As our line of craft approached the shore the Navy's guns were blazing and smashing shells into fortifications.

"Just ahead of us tank landing craft were already inshore and tanks were racing up the shingle. German 88 millimetre guns got on to them and there were several direct hits which knocked out the tanks. Others came on.

"We had no time to see how they got on as our craft were by this time bumping on to the beach. Three hundred yards ahead of us was a high concrete wall about 20ft high. Jerries were lining the top, sweeping with their machine-guns and hurling hand-grenades as we swept forward.

"Several of our lads fell but we dashed forward and got under the base of the wall where the Jerries couldn't get at us. More of our landing craft were coming inshore.

"I took a glimpse backward and saw one go up in flames. It had hit one of their underwater obstructions.

"I had seen these sticking up out of the water as we came in, but we missed them. They were long ramps sticking up from the sea bottom, intended to rip the bottoms out of our craft."

▶ Two Allied soldiers, casualties of the Normandy landings, smoke a cigarette after disembarking from the hospital ship.

SINKING, GOT TANKS ASHORE

MEN ON LANDING CRAFT BALED WITH BUCKETS AND PANS TO REACH LAND

Knee-deep in water aboard a holed and sinking tank landing craft, sailors and soldiers feverishly baled with buckets, pans – everything they could lay their hands on – in their determination to get the craft, with its precious cargo of tanks, to the French shore, only a few hundred yards away.

The story is told by Desmond Tighe, Reuter special correspondent aboard the destroyer *Beagle*, who watched the landing craft, towed by a small minesweeper, pass close by.

"I don't know who the young skipper of the landing craft was," he says, "but if any man had done his job properly in the assault, he certainly had."

Describing the beach battle as he saw it from the *Beagle*, Tighe says: "Away to the south-west British destroyers are bombarding. Through our glasses we can see German tanks deploying on the beaches just below the sea wall.

"A stubborn battery on the cliff tops, just to the right, keeps up intermittent fire, and the shells are sending up large sprays of water

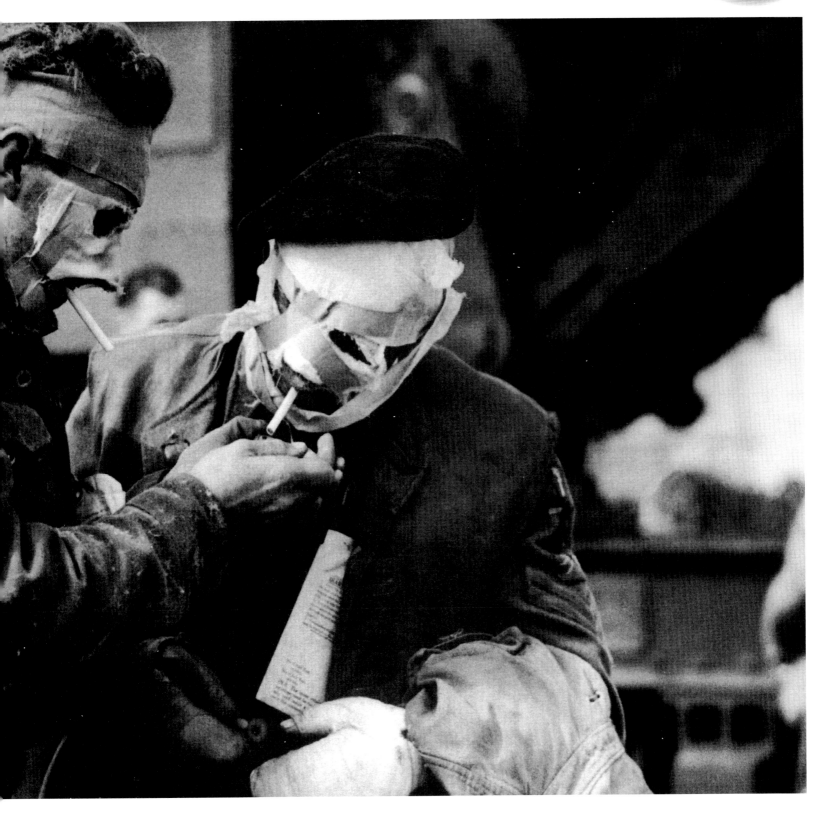

Wounded British soldiers read news from the front as they return to England from France.

◀ Field-Marshal Montgomery and the Prime Minister inspect the Normandy
beachhead in the days after the invasion of Northern France.

round the destroyers.

"But the destroyers fight on like greyhounds, darting in and plastering the enemy gun positions.

"Inland pillars of smoke show where stubborn artillery battles are being fought.

"The climax came when we watched the second wave of glider-borne troops soaring in over the area. They came in hundreds in one endless stream, flying incredibly low.

"The sky was black with them. As the navigating officer said: 'They look like birds migrating to the Continent.'"

THE MAN WHO KNEW THE DATE

Major-General Henry Miller, commander of the Ninth Air Force Service Command in Britain since October last year, was reduced to the rank of lieutenant-colonel and sent back to the United States for disclosing the invasion date at a cocktail party, it is revealed by Supreme Command. His conversation took place more than two months ago, when the invasion was expected almost daily.

In the presence of several guests, he said: "On my honour, the invasion takes place before June 13."

The story was withheld because it was feared that enemy agents would trace back the cocktail party and find out exactly what he said.

MICKEY MOUSE WAS NAVY HIGH-UPS' D-DAY PASSWORD

Senior naval officers passing into a naval cinema at a southern port a few days before the invasion, had to whisper into the ear of the sentry the words "Mickey Mouse."

They weren't going to see a film, but to be briefed for invasion operations.

They learned for the first time where the landings were to take place, and there was a buzz of surprise as an enormous map was unrolled. The briefing went on all day and each time an officer left or re-entered the cinema he had to say "Mickey Mouse."

PUP FIRST "CASUALTY"

By YOUR SPECIAL CORRESPONDENT

NELLIE, three-month-old mongrel pup . . . may not have two tails to be proud of, but she can certainly wag her only one with justifiable pride.

For she took part in D-Day – watching operations from the deck of one of the many motor torpedo-boats covering the landings.

But that is not all. She also made history by being the first invasion "casualty" landed on the South Coast.

The crew were undecided whether or not to take Nellie. But when they saw Nellie's appealing look no one could say "no."

So she went. But when she arrived back at port she ran up on to the jetty, sat down, and became ill.

Three Wrens came to Nellie's rescue and gave her a meal and a bath.

"We hope to keep Nellie," one of them told the *Daily Mirror* yesterday.

◗ Churchill chats to a platoon of British soldiers while inspecting the Normandy beachhead six days after the D-Day landings.

The Battle of Normandy

June – August **1944**

Getting ashore was only the beginning. Staying ashore and then making progress inland was a different story. The landings themselves succeeded partly through the element of surprise, with the Germans fully expecting the Allies to choose the area around Calais as their target. Once Hitler directed his forces further west, the Allies had a fight on their hands. It took a month to oust the Germans from Caen, only a few miles inland. And it was not until the middle of August that Montgomery's men reached the Seine. But once Paris was liberated the march eastwards became almost a stampede.

◄ French children play in a pool on the beach at Arromanches while a ship discharges its cargo to awaiting troops.

SECOND ROUND BATTLES RAGE

ALLIED FORCES MEETING BIG HUN CHALLENGE

THE Allied infantry and tanks which thrust inland from the Normandy beachheads are now fighting out the second crucial phase of the invasion assault.

Heavy battles raged yesterday as Montgomery's forces, backed by mighty air support, met the challenge of Rommel's first-string reserves – the enemy troops placed just outside the invasion areas and now being thrown into action.

The first phase fighting is over – the securing of a foothold on the Continent and the defeat of the German coast defenders. Airborne troops have in some places linked up with the seaborne forces, and reinforcements are being steadily moved in to the beachheads.

The second phase fighting now going on is to consolidate our gains. Only by success in a third phase – the engagement and defeat of the enemy's main, strategic reserves – will we be able to make substantial advances.

Berlin stated last night that Allied infantry and big forces of tanks, fed from a thirty-one-mile-wide beachhead, were thrusting out on both sides of the captured town of Bayeux to link up with airborne troops in the Caen area to the south-east, and the Carentan area, at the foot of the Cherbourg Peninsula.

Allied medium bombers and fighters yesterday ranged over the Cherbourg Peninsula and the roads leading to it, attacking road hubs and bridges. To the south, heavy bombers blasted major airfield and rail targets in a deep zone.

To the east, the city of Caen was attacked by medium bombers which left great fires in their wake.

The Luftwaffe is now moving planes from Germany to the west. Increased opposition to the Allied air fleets has begun.

◖ Lorries and jeeps drive off a Mulberry harbour at Gold Beach in Normandy. More than 8,000 men worked for eight months to build these floating harbours vital to the Allied cause.

18 – WOUNDED

Home from the invasion battle 18-year-old Geoffrey Smith, Beverley, Yorks, an Army volunteer at 17, is telling a comrade how he was wounded:

"Yesterday was my big moment. I got clear of the assault craft, waded through the water, and rushed up the beach at Caen with my rifle at the ready.

"Then I saw a group of Germans behind a machine-gun. It was pointing at me. I saw the smoke round the muzzle, then there was a terrible pain in my arm and I fell down."

Geoffrey says he saw concrete pill-boxes, pit timbers sticking up from the beach – everywhere signs of determined fortifications, but very few Germans.

18—wounded

THE FIRST TOWN TO
BE FREED

"WE have waited for this day."

The cry – heard over and over – voiced the feelings of the people who greeted the Allied troops when they occupied Bayeux.

But there was no joyous French abandon in their greeting.

Here, in Bayeux – the first town to be freed – one felt that the people had really suffered – not only for a matter of a few days or weeks – but continuously and cumulatively through four long years.

You felt it in their shy, nervous approach, just as surely as you marked it in the hollow cheeks of the women, and the pathetically spindly legs of their children.

Like a people who had been frozen by suffering during these years, they had first to thaw – to realise the implications of freedom.

But they were ready. There were very few men – and almost none of these was of military age – but the women and children made the V sign and every child carried a little bouquet of flowers.

The moment the jeeps and tanks stopped they surrounded them. They did not speak rapidly or easily. The women and the few men thrust forward their hands and grasped those of the troops, and the children presented their posies.

Then, from moment to moment, one could feel the atmosphere warming. Magically, they produced bottles of wine and glasses.

Our men solemnly pledged France, Britain and America. But the French people's toasts were grimmer – to the destruction of Germany and the death of Hitler.

➡ British troops serve food to the people of Bayeux after liberating the Normandy town. Produce from the area had been sent to Germany and Paris but was now available for local use.

German prisoners of war disembark from a landing craft in England and begin the march to a prison camp.

THE PRISONERS STILL COMING

Some of the first group of German prisoners captured disembark at a British port yesterday.

Displaying every emotion from arrogance to bewilderment they marched to waiting trucks with armed guard and were then moved to an unknown destination.

British soldiers in Normandy look for souvenirs to send back home.

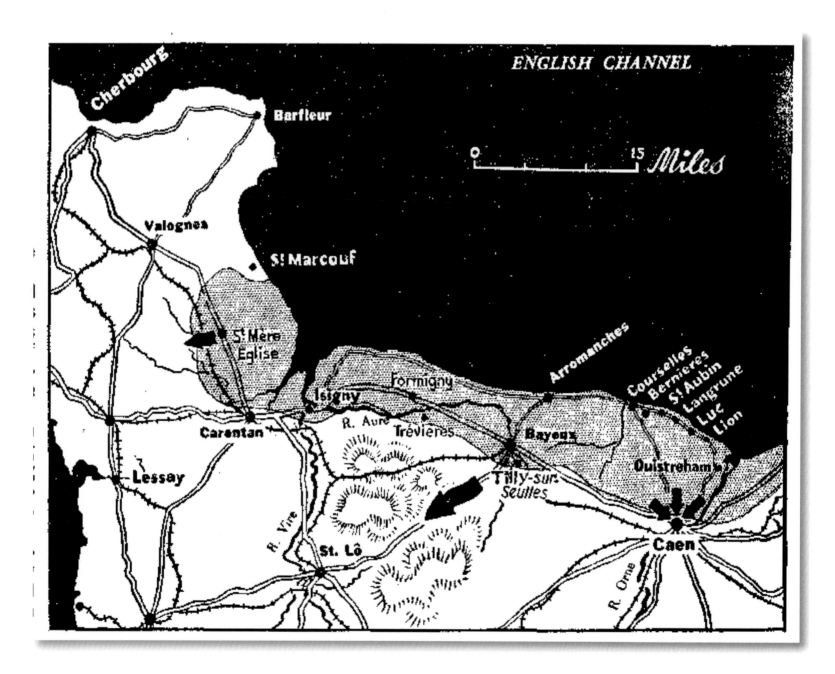

12 June 1944

OUR FORCES HOLD UNBROKEN LINE OF 51 MILES

WITH the fighting around our invasion bridgehead becoming heavier hourly the Allied forces continue to widen their grip on Normandy.

An outstanding feature of the fighting is the terrific intensity of our air assaults on the Germans' gun emplacements and supply columns. Our air supremacy becomes more and more marked each day. Marauders, which formerly bombed from medium heights, are now sweeping the countryside at the hitherto unheard of altitude of 200ft., playing havoc with their heavy-calibre machine-guns, and the enemy can do nothing about it.

The Luftwaffe has been afraid to commit itself even at night. A barrage from ships and shore batteries almost as heavy as London's greets every German plane which approaches the beachhead, while swarms of night fighters, both 2nd Tactical Air Force and Air Defence of Great Britain, are ready to shoot them out of the skies.

▶ Allied soldiers take cover during the bombing of German positions along the Caen–Falaise road.

▶ British tanks and armour pass through Falaise, which has been left burning by German incendiaries and RAF bombing.

28 June 1944

BIG NEW DRIVE NEAR CAEN AS CHERBOURG FALLS

BRITISH HURL HUNS BACK

WITH Cherbourg in the Allies' hands, the British forces who launched their great attack towards the Villers-Bocage–Caen main road have delivered a smashing blow to the heavy German armour and infantry and advanced several miles.

They have captured the villages of St Maurieu, Le Gaule and Le Haut de Bosq, as well as securing Cheux Fontenay.

Our forces yesterday were within two miles of the vital road they aimed at, thus tending to make a sweep round the west of the enemy key pivot at Caen.

The British assault was delivered under the greatest barrage yet seen in Normandy. As thousands of shells hurtled into the enemy positions our infantry, supported by tanks, drove forward into

the thickly-wooded country and within a few hours had entered several villages.

Fierce close-quarter fighting from house to house took place before the Germans were finally routed out from these places.

🔺 French civilians push their bicycles past Allied troops in Normandy.

FOURTH FRONT

THE war makes good progress on all four fronts. Cherbourg is ours; the first naval stronghold and deep water port to be recaptured on this side and a great asset for the campaign in France. Montgomery now begins his main assault on the enemy forces. These events coincide with the Russian offensive, which is completely successful, and in some places incredibly rapid. In Italy, Alexander, despite stiff opposition in places, proceeds steadily towards his objective, which is the destruction of Kesselring's armies. There remains the Fourth Front – the South of England

Front – where civilians, men, women and children, are once more in the firing line. This area of hostilities is entitled to be called a Front because it is having a much more important effect on the war than the Germans ever imagined. In order to make these Buzz Bombs the Germans have had to divert skilled labour and material from the manufacture of other types of aircraft, particularly fighters. This accounts for the shortage of aerial opposition in Normandy. And what is the result? Prisoners taken in Normandy during the last few days complain bitterly that, owing to the claims of the new missile, they have been denied the air cover they have a right to expect when engaged in heavy fighting. Constantly exposed to attacks by Allied air forces, they seldom see a sign of the Luftwaffe in the sky.

The Buzz Bomb is a retaliatory weapon. It is intended to be a morale buster. But the morale it is likely to bust is not ours but that of the German soldiers fighting in Europe. The Fourth Front is, therefore, playing a proud and useful part. It is being of direct advantage to our men in the thick of the fight.

There is no weak link.

The end approached. Hitler launched his flying-bombs in swarms on battered South-eastern England. But London could still take it.

(July 4, 1944)

61

Cartoonist Philip Zec captures the indomitable spirit of the British, standing up to the German buzz bombs on southern England.

More than 200 Guardsmen and their friends were at a parade service in the 106-year-old Guards' Chapel, at Wellington Barracks, London, when a buzz bomb crashed on the building and left it a wreck like this.

When the cloud of dust settled, and there was no further need for heroism in the debris, the rescuers paused, and noticed that the altar was practically undamaged, and still shining above it was the legend: "Glory to God . . . Be thou faithful unto death, and I will give thee a crown of life."

(It was here that Lieut.-Colonel Lord Edward Hay, Grenadier Guards, and Major Causley Windram, Senior Director of Music of the Brigade of Guards, and many others were killed).

A German POW sits with his head in his hand in a barbed wire enclosure in Normandy.

29 June **1944**

FIRST 15 DAYS: 1,842 BRITISH TROOPS KILLED

THE number of British troops killed in Normandy in the first fifteen days of the fighting was 1,842, with 8,599 wounded and 3,131 missing, a total of 13,572.

Many of the men reported missing are bound to turn up.

The total Allied casualties in the fifteen-day period was 40,549, including 5,287 killed.

Detailed figures for the Americans and Canadians are:

United States. – 3,082 killed, 13,121 wounded, 7,959 missing; total 24.162.

Canadian. – 363 killed, 1,359 wounded, 1,093 missing; total 2,815.

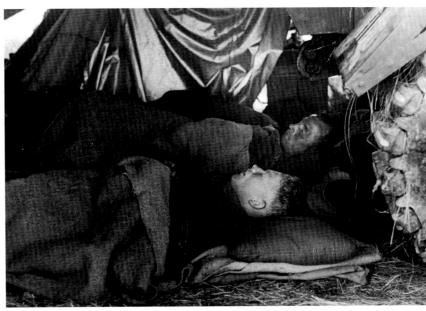

A British tank crew rests, sleeping under the protection of their vehicle.

More than a quarter of the aggregate casualties represent missing men.

German casualties were much greater in the first fortnight, and a rough conservative estimate of the enemy losses for the first twenty-one days is 90,000 killed, wounded and missing.

Latest figure of the prisoners taken by the Americans in the Cherbourg Peninsula is between 30,000 and 40,000.

Canadian troops rest under a hedge in the Normandy countryside following bitter close-quarter combat with German forces.

10 July **1944**

MONTY'S TWIN VICTORY OVER ROMMEL

BRITISH TROOPS SEIZE CAEN

By GEORGE McCARTHY,
outside Caen, Sunday

BRITISH troops are in the centre of Caen. They have reached the northern bank of the river in strength.

The battle began early yesterday with an air bombardment by over 400 Lancasters and Halifaxes. At 4.30 a.m. our artillery opened fire. The battle raged all day yesterday. By nightfall we had captured most of the villages to the west, but pockets of Germans remained to the north.

Last night our armour broke into the northern outskirts. They found the roads heavily cratered and mined and withdrew.

This morning our troops thrust back into the streets. Our heavy air bombing must have devastated strongpoints also on the north side of the river, and it was thought that the Germans might have been forced to the south bank on the River Orne.

But today and during the night our patrols found the Germans fighting hard for the northern half of the town.

They had prepared positions in the debris and hastily dug slit trenches.

FEW SNIPERS LEFT

It seemed that the enemy was going to fight for the streets and the houses.

But by late this afternoon street fighting in the northern suburbs has died down and few snipers are left in the houses.

I am writing this in a village church on the edge of the battlefield.

There is no service this Sunday, but then there are no worshippers. The spire has a shell hole through it, but the interior is undamaged, its walls still hung with pictures that tell the story of the life and death of Christ.

Outside, the British guns are booming and British troops are patrolling. There is little German reply, although the enemy mortaring has only recently stopped and the walls and fields testify to his activities.

German prisoners are coming in steadily. Among them was a Persian, who knew almost no German.

One declared that the British soldier was fighting a cowardly battle because his infantry equipment was so much better than the German.

◆ An Allied soldier leads German prisoners, many of whom were from the Hitler Youth Division, captured during the battle for Caen.

German prisoners captured by American soldiers on the march near Cherbourg in June 1944.

German troops surrender to American soldiers in Cherbourg in June 1944.

Early this morning destroyers on patrol sighted and chased a force of five armed trawlers off Cape Frehel. The enemy force escaped inshore under shelter of shore batteries, but not before they had received serious punishment.

◀ Winston Churchill has his cigar lit by a local on a tour of Cherbourg in July 1944.

2 August 1944

BERLIN SAYS "OUR NORMANDY LINE ENGULFED"

ALLIES SMASH HUN FLANK

U.S. CAPTURE 7,800 MORE, KILL 4,500 – AND DRIVE ON

U.S. tanks last night smashed and turned the German left flank and broke out of the Cherbourg Peninsula, transforming the Battle of Normandy into the opening of the Battle of France.

On the rest of the line curving north-east, British and American forces stormed into the string of enemy key points – Villedieu, Percy and Tessy – and cracked the centre with a deep wedge south-west of Caumont.

The German High Command reported a crisis in these words:

"Our troops will now have to face tasks of utmost difficulty in view of the fact that the entire front has been engulfed by the British and American offensive."

Berlin radio reported "disengagement movements" owing to a deep penetration – admission that the German flank was being rolled up from the west.

GENERAL BRADLEY'S H.Q. REVEALED THAT ON MONDAY 7,812 PRISONERS WERE TAKEN BY THE AMERICANS, AND THAT 4,500 GERMANS WERE KILLED IN A POCKET WHICH WAS SEALED SOUTH OF COUTANCES, MILES BEHIND THE SPEARHEADS.

In a week the U.S. forces have taken 18,587 prisoners, bringing

COMMUNIQUÉ

GENERAL EISENHOWER'S midnight communiqué announced:

The town of Caen has been liberated.

Many pockets of enemy resistance remain, but these are being systematically dealt with. Local gains have been made in the Odon bridgehead and in the Caumont-Tilly sector.

German resistance in La Haye du Puits was crushed after the town had been bypassed on both sides.

Some ground has also been gained towards Sainteny, although enemy resistance is intense both in this area and beyond St. Jean de Daye.

their total since D-Day to 69,000. Seven enemy divisions have been destroyed.

£50,000 ON HIS HEAD: "HE TRIED TO MURDER HITLER"

A REWARD of £50,000 has been offered in Germany for the capture of a man named as a conspirator in the alleged attempt on Hitler's life.

He is Dr. Karl Goerdeler, former Mayor of Leipzig, who seems to have beaten the grand round-up by the Gestapo.

German radio announced the reward in the following statement:
"WANTED FOR MURDER:

Major Karl Goerdeler for conspiracy against the life of the Fuehrer. Reward 1,000,000 marks [about £50,000 at prewar rates].

"Dr. A.D. Karl Goerdeler has since disappeared. He was born at Schneidemuehl, Prussia, on July 31, 1884. His last residence was Leipzig."

Dr. Goerdeler is the first prominent German politician to be named officially in connection with the plot.

➤ British troops survey the remains of vehicles and supplies left by the German Army on the banks of the River Seine.

American troops make their way through a bomb-damaged Normandy town.

An American soldier lies dead after the battle for Saint-Lô.

FRONT LINE TO SEE FILM PREMIERE

By YOUR SPECIAL CORRESPONDENT

TROOPS in the Normandy battle area are to see the first front-line world film premiere next Tuesday.

Film to be screened for them is "Casanova Brown," starring forty-four-year-old Gary Cooper and Theresa Wright. It is to be shown simultaneously in sixteen liberated towns.

Distinguished guests will be there all right, some of the greatest men and women in the world – the British and American troops now cracking the Huns, with the girls in the auxiliary Services, nurses, doctors and others.

The cinemas will be lorries, barns, halls with their roofs blown off, or any old thing which can take a portable screen and projector.

The Tommies, Doughboys and Servicewomen in their battle dresses will see "Casanova Brown" some six months before any British civilian will have a chance of seeing Gary and Theresa in their second team-up since they starred together in "Pride of the Yankees."

◆ British infantry rush past the burning remains of a farmhouse south of Le Bény-Bocage that the Germans had been using as a base.

25 August 1944

ENGLAND'S SEASIDE IS FREE TO ALL: LAST BAN IS LIFTED

YOU may go to the seaside anywhere in England to day.

There are no longer any special defence areas other than to which aliens alone are denied admittance.

The lifting of the ban on the remaining restricted areas from the Wash to Lymington, Hants, was announced by the War Office last night.

These areas will remain regulated areas however. This means that should the need arise, the military authorities can deny to the public access to some specified spot or district or highway.

Identity cards must always be carried in public places, and telescopes and binoculars must not be used anywhere in these areas.

Certain beaches are, however, still closed to the public because they are unsafe owing to mines. It is expected that they will be few.

➡ A man and his children walk through a ruined French town in August 1944.

IT'S A RACE TO SAVE BRAVE MEN

From GEORGE McCARTHY,
Rambouillet, Thursday

IT is, after all, to be a fight for Paris.

At one o'clock yesterday the B.B.C. announced that the men of the Maquis had liberated the capital. It was not entirely untrue, but in the afternoon the Germans returned in strength with tanks and armoured cars.

And while the Allied armies are held outside the gates, the streets of the capital are running with blood. The blood of Frenchmen fighting to be free.

The facts are that the hard-pressed men of the Maquis are now calling on the Allied armies for help. And the advancing American

and French troops have still to battle their way through a German rearguard screen to the south of Versailles.

And against that rearguard line the Americans are today throwing their armour and their infantry.

It is a race to save the valiant men of the Maquis from the vengeance of the now desperate Germans. I hope England realises the debt we owe these fighting Frenchmen – these bands of boys who pit their ill-assorted arms against the might of the surviving German armour.

It is heartbreaking to be sitting here thirty miles from Paris in the knowledge that the mighty Allied army cannot yet reach the men of the Paris streets.

It is not for lack of local encouragement. The road from Chartres to Rambouillet has been the way of a conqueror.

In every village and hamlet the old men, the girls and the women have lined the roadside to cheer.

And always the cry has been "To Paris."

◀ Citizens of Courseulles-sur-Mer, north of Caen, read public notices put up by the Allied military authorities.

'MAGAZINE PAGE' GIRL

Mlle. Simone, the 19-year-old Maquis. Over her shoulder is the British Sten gun with which she has killed two Germans and captured twenty-five others.

Simone, one of General de Gaulle's guard of honour at Chartres on Wednesday, when he pronounced the city free, was described by George McCarthy, *Daily Mirror* chief correspondent, as looking "like the front page girl of a coloured magazine."

⬥ British troops talk to a local gendarme in a Normandy town.

26 August 1944

EVERY LANE A GERMAN DEATH TRAP

Streets, lanes and roads on the German escape routes from the Falaise Gap to the Seine are choked like this with the battered debris of trucks, tanks and guns, relentlessly strafed by rocket-firing Typhoons and other aircraft loosed above the stampede.

Debris and the dead are strewn over miles of the countryside. Ditches are black with German helmets.

Allied maps were marked simply "Killing Corner." The soldiers left it to the destroying airmen, and correspondents spoke of their "awestruck horror" at the consequences.

🔺 Winston Churchill, Field-Marshal Montgomery and Viscount Alanbrooke inspect a line of tank traps.

◆ Allied troops in Paris.

28 August **1944**

"AT LAST" CRIED PARIS AS THE ALLIES ARRIVED

From GEORGE McCARTHY, Daily Mirror Chief Correspondent,
Paris, Saturday

WE are in Paris. The way has been a conqueror's triumphal progress.

I type this in the street Denfert Rochereau in the 14th district of the capital. And around me are the people of Paris watching this and spelling out the words as I write.

They have shaken my hands, they have embraced me and all have cried: "At last, at last."

For a week now I have waited outside Paris and I have tried to tell these enthusiastic street audiences how long I have waited. They cry in chorus: "But we have waited four years."

Now the men of the resistance are patrolling the streets in armoured cars and on foot.

Here, in this district, the last Germans have been driven off,

but sniping still goes on. The soldiers of the Maquis are pointing their rifles to the roofs, firing there, where the last hidden Germans remain.

They have been short of food for weeks in the capital, but there is so far little sign of starvation.

The people now around me explain that it has been specially bad for the poor. They could not buy in the black market that flourished under the noses of the Germans.

French tanks now are rolling down the street and the people cheer the maroon caps of their own men. But they are in no doubt as to who has won the laurels.

The battle of the streets of Paris has been won by these bands of ragged soldiers, the civilian army that fought for De Gaulle and for France.

That battle is not yet over. Gunfire still sounds in the streets. There is fierce fighting in the area of the Senate. But here we are cheering for France and for England, the Allies in arms again.

Now the joy of Paris has reached a crescendo. The men and women and children are clapping their hands and cheering every French and American truck and tank to drive down the lined streets.

Each vehicle is wreathed in flowers for, in every village and hamlet on the way in, the people have turned out to throw bouquets of red, white and blue.

Indeed, our jeep arrived looking like a harvest festival, for in one village men and women poured baskets of delicious tomatoes into our hands and pelted us again with flowers.

And now Paris is enjoying its great day. An old woman in tears has been clutching at my sleeve to convince herself that a dream has come true – the English are here. Young women have rushed up to kiss and embrace me again and always they shout "at last, at last."

A special edition of the *Figaro* is on the streets with the headlines, "The liberation of Paris, the last day in the chains."

It reports how the hard-pressed men of the resistance had been told that help was on the way.

Then the tanks appeared and they ran forward expecting to greet Americans.

Instead French troops jumped from the tanks and the men of the resistance were joyfully embracing their countrymen.

CHEVALIER KILLED BY PATRIOTS

FRENCH patriots say that they have killed Maurice Chevalier, the former French film idol and cabaret star. They killed him on Friday.

Chevalier was a collaborator. He had been known as such ever

since the French armistice in 1940. He was 55.

Maurice, of the embracing grin, the gamin impudence, and the straw hat, was the comic star of the revues at the Casino de Paris, the man who made £200,000, a year even in 1930, when the world was sewn up in depression.

The Dominion Theatre in London once guaranteed him a £4,000 a week minimum.

Hollywood gave him all he asked for as the star of "The Love Parade", with Jeannette MacDonald.

He never offended the Germans. They asked him to sing in Berlin, and he did.

22 November **1944**

MAURICE CHEVALIER NOT A COLLABORATOR

Maurice Chevalier, the stage and screen star who had been suspected of "collaborationist activity" during the occupation, has been given a clean bill by the French music hall's purge committee.

In its official statement the committee said Chevalier gave one entertainment only at a German prison camp. He was not paid and ten prisoners were released in exchange for his services.

⬧ The French capital gets back to normal after its liberation from the Nazis.

American anti-aircraft guns guard the bridges over the Seine.

Destination Berlin

The race was on. The German armies were in retreat in the east and west; the Russians and Allies were both marching on Berlin. Who would get there first? But there were still obstacles to overcome. V-1 bombs were raining down on Southern England from the French and Belgian coast, so the Allies had to secure that area, and German resistance along the Siegfried Line remained a serious threat to the Allied advance.

◀ Belgian citizens welcome British troops to Brussels by jumping on a British tank and riding through the city.

2 mths. HUNS TOLD, WIPE OUT GAINS OF 2 yrs.

30 August 1944

2 MTHS. HUNS TOLD, WIPE OUT GAINS OF 2 YRS.

GERMAN radio commentator Dittmar admitted to the German people last night that in two months the Germans have lost the greater part of what it took them two years to conquer.

"We must not conceal to the German people the seriousness of our position," he declared.

"The times of sweeping successes lie far behind us. The greater part of France has slipped out of our hands."

31 August 1944

BOMB PRATTLE

LET us try to get the position clear as regards the bombardment of what the authorities still absurdly call "Southern England." In his last review of the war the Prime Minister himself expressed the opinion that this ordeal was likely to continue for some time, and he counselled all who could do so to leave the London area. The result has been evacuation on a considerable scale, not only of mothers and children but of organisations. The Ministry of Health supplemented Mr. Churchill's advice by prompt efficient action and, as a result, a big job has been successfully performed. Is there, at the present time, any solid basis of fact, by reason of which the official attitude in this matter can be safely disregarded?

Everyone, naturally, is anxious to see the last of the flying bomb, but those in high positions render a poor service by confusing the public mind. One day we are treated to optimistic forecasts, the next, the bombs reach us in more than average profusion. Bomb sites are captured; General Pile explains to visitors the complex mechanism of defence; Sir Ernest Gowers, Regional Commissioner, expresses the view that we are not only in the "final phase" of the flying bomb battle, but that this final phase is "nearing its end." Cheering words. We hope they are true. In the meantime people in the danger zone do not know how to act. Some, who have already gone away, are seeking to return; others, on the point of departure, decide to "take a chance" and stay on. Meanwhile the sirens continue to sound; the bombs come hurtling over and there is no guarantee that worse is not to come. The one fact is that the danger is not yet ended, and until Government assurance on that point can be given the only sensible thing to do is to continue every possible precaution.

2 September 1944

MONTY'S MEN PAST ARRAS IN BUZZ-COAST PURSUIT

ALLIES REACH BELGIUM

ALLIED tanks have reached the Belgian frontier north of Sedan.

Field-Marshal Montgomery's armour has raced thirty-five miles from Amiens and passed Arras, only thirty miles from Belgium, in hustling the disorganised Germans from the buzz-bomb coast.

Other Allied tanks, storming east across the River Meuse at captured Verdun, are believed to be within forty miles of the German frontier.

Those sensational advances were reported by Allied war correspondents last night.

Monty's spearheads have thrust north and north-west of Amiens at whirlwind speed through country where, more than anywhere else, each mile of advance means one buzz-bomb less.

Little resistance is being met, and any of the strongpoints held by the Germans are being bypassed and mopped up by following waves of lorried infantry.

DIEPPE RAIDERS GO BACK: NOT A SHOT

CANADIAN units which took part in the Dieppe raid two years ago captured the city from the landward side yesterday without firing a shot.

They drove through streets where on that rehearsal for invasion they saw their comrades mown down.

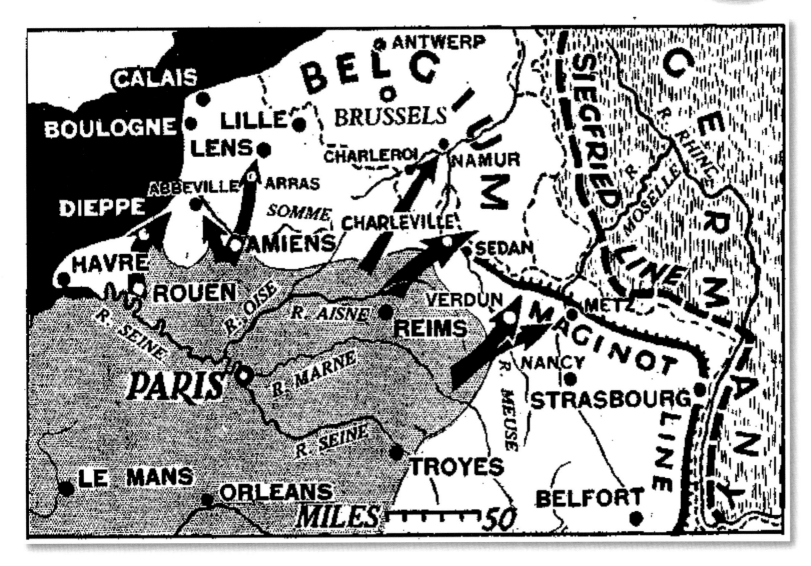

But now the avenues of death were filled with a welcoming people. They were greeted, not with bullets, but with flowers.

They were the Essex Scottish the Royal Hamilton Light Infantry and the Royal Regiment of Canada, all units of the Second Canadian Division.

Following them were other Dieppe units – the South Saskatchewan Regiment, the Black Watch and the Toronto Scottish.

The city itself is not badly damaged, although the Germans, who are believed to have pulled out on Thursday night, carried out considerable demolitions and put all the public utilities out of commission.

The Canadian troops driving on Dieppe took some prisoners but these were the only Germans encountered in the dash from Rouen.

Dieppe was the scene of the first Allied pre-invasion landing in strength. Carried out on August 19, 1942, its aim was to test the German defences and Allied tactics.

Canadian shock troops formed five-sixths of the assault forces. A British Commando unit under Lord Lovat also took part.

The troops stayed nine hours on shore and were then disembarked, the raid having cost about 2,000 men in killed and prisoners.

4 September 1944

MAPS BY TON

Ten tons of maps of Germany were dropped by parachute on

BOMBEN ÜBER DEUTSCHLAND — bis 5. Oktober

In den auf dieser Karte dargestellten Städten wurden militärische Objekte durch die britische Luftwaffe bombardiert. Die Bombenangriffe werden immer umfangreicher.

Das nachstehende Städteverzeichnis ist nur eine Auslese. Die Ziffern bedeuten die Zahl der auf die einzelnen Städte bis 5. Oktober stattgefundenen Bombenangriffe.

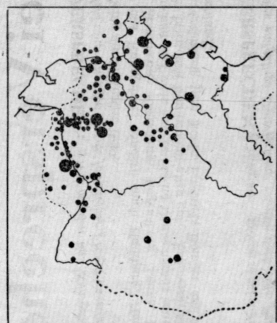

ZEICHENERKLÄRUNG

(betr. die zerstörten oder beschädigten militärischen Ziele):

F—Flugplätze, Flughäfen für Seeflugzeuge, Flugzeugfabriken, Flugzeuglager

S—Kriegshäfen, Stützpunkte der Kriegsmarine, Docks, Landungsplätze, Häfen, Hafendämme, Kanäle, Schiffswerfte, Boote

T—Öl-, Petroleum- und Benzinlager, Raffinerien, Tanks, Fabrikanlagen der Treibstoffproduktion

B—Bahnlinien, Knotenpunkte, Rangier- und Güterbahnhöfe, Verladungsplätze

W—Munitionsbetriebe, Hochöfen, chemische Werke, Kraft-(Elektrizitäts)werke

M—Munitionslager

Unter den zerstörten oder schwer beschädigten kriegswichtigen Betrieben befinden sich:

Bayer Sprengstoffwerke (Leverkusen), Bayrische Motorenwerke (München), Blohm u. Voss Werft (Hamburg), Bosch Akkumulatoren (Stuttgart), Daimler-Benz (Stuttgart), Deutsche Schiffs-u. Maschinenbau (Bremen), Dornier (Wenzendorf und Wismar), Fieseler (Kassel), I. G. Farben (Leuna), Junkers (Bernburg und Dessau), Krupp (Essen), Messerschmitt (Gotha und Augsburg), Mockau-Erla (Leipzig), Rheinische Kraftwerke (Köln), Siemens u. Schuckert (Berlin), Zeiss (Jena).

Ort	Ziel	Bombenangriffe	Ort	Ziel	Bombenangriffe
Aachen	F B	7	Kastrop-Rauxel	T	3
Augsburg	F	2	Keltersbach	W	1
Berlin	F T B W	17	Kiel	S T	18
Bernburg	F	2	Kochem	W	1
Bitterfeld	W	2	Kölleda	F	1
Bohlen	T	1	Köln	F T B W	33
Bonn	F B	4	Krefeld	F B M	13
Borkum	F	10	Leipzig	F W	3
Bottrop	T	5	Leuna	T	3
Bremen	F S T B	32	Leverkusen	W	4
Bremerhaven	S	3	Lippstadt	B W	2
Cuxhaven	F S	4	Lingen	F B	4
Deichshausen	F T	5	Ludwigshafen	T B W	9
Dessau	F	3	Lünen	B W	6
Diepholz	F	6	Magdeburg	F T B W	11
Dortmund	F T B W M	14	Mannheim	T B	17
Dortmund-Ems-Kanal	-	11	Monheim	T W	11
Duisburg	S B	13	Misburg	T	4
Düsseldorf	F T W	7	München	F	1
Ehrang	B	11	Münster	F B	7
Emden	S T M	19	Nordenham	T	2
Emmerich	S T B	9	Norderney	F S	14
Eschwege	F	5	Osnabrück	B M	22
Essen	B W	17	Osterfeld	B M	2
Frankfurt	T W	12	Paderborn	F M	5
Finkenherd	W	1	Pölitz	T	3
Gelsenkirchen	B T W	20	Quakenbrück	T	3
Gladbach	B W	4	Regensburg	T	1
Gotha	F	3	Reisholz	T W	5
Göttingen	F	2	Rheinberg	F	1
Grevenbroich	W	2	Recklinghausen	B	2
Griesheim	W		Rheine	B M	5
Hamborn	F S		Rotenburg	F	4
Hamburg	S T				
Hamm	B M				
Hannover	F T				
Helgoland	S M				
Höchst	W				
Homberg	T B				
Hornum	F W				
Huntlosen	F W				
Jena	W T B				
Kamen	T B				
Kassel	F W				

TERROR !

TERROR war Hitlers Waffe als er das deutsche Volk und Reich seiner Partei dienstbar machte.

TERROR war Hitlers Waffe gegen Österreich, die Tschechoslowakei, Polen, Norwegen, Terror gegen Wehrlose, Mord an Waffenlosen, Brandstiftung an unverteidigten Städten.

TERROR hemmungsloser, vorbedachter Terror zwang Holland, Belgien und das uneinige Frankreich auf die Kniee.

TERROR sollte auch Englands Kampfeswillen brechen. Aber

Ihr habt Euch verrechnet!

Gegen die sprichwörtliche Gleichmütigkeit, gegen die eisernen Nerven, gegen den sturen Willen der Briten vermögen Görings Bomben nichts. Tag für Tag wird Euch diese Lehre deutlicher beigebracht.

BOMBEN WIDER BOMBEN !

Das ist unsere Antwort an Hitler: Bomben und immer mehr Bomben.

BOMBEN auf die Kasernen, auf die Kriegshäfen, auf die Flugplätze.

BOMBEN auf die Kruppwerke, auf Spandau, auf Augsburg, auf Magdeburg.

BOMBEN auf alle Benzinfabriken, auf Leuna, Misburg, Pölitz.

BOMBEN auf die deutsche Kriegsmaschine. Bomben immer tiefer nach Osten hinein.

WIR SCHLAGEN ZURÜCK !

438

Saturday night to Allied troops advancing: towards the south-west frontier of the Reich.

The maps were flown to a forward area in response to an urgent request, ordinary transport being too slow to catch up with the advance.

Leaflets warning Germans where bombs would be targeted were dropped by RAF planes.

♦ British forces enter Valkenswenswaard, the first Dutch village to be liberated.

BRITISH TANKS SWEEP ON TO HOLLAND

SPEARHEADS of General Dempsey's army were last night approaching the frontier of Holland after their lightning advance into and beyond Brussels.

Before midday yesterday they had reached within twenty-five miles of the Dutch border.

An unconfirmed report from the French frontier said, "The Allies have entered Antwerp."

"It's more of a hell-for-leather race than a fight," commented a correspondent.

With most of Belgium ours without a battle, Holland looks like going the same way.

➤ A British Army dispatch rider stuck in the mud gets a helping hand from a Dutch boy.

◀ Crowds gather and cheer as British tanks pass through Brussels.

7 September **1944**

60,000 HUNS IN BUZZ-COAST TRAP

ALLIED UNITS ENTER REICH

ALLIED troops have crossed the German frontier, it was announced yesterday.

Patrols of the U.S. Third Army entered Germany on September 3rd, fifth anniversary of Britain's declaration of war, it was revealed.

They established a bridgehead over the Moselle River, ranged for a few miles on German territory, and then withdrew.

Troops which had earlier entered Luxembourg seem to have made the reconnaissance into Germany. They had some days ago been reported to have reached the little German town of Perl, just over the Luxembourg border.

Official silence was preserved yesterday on the exact position of the Third Army troops facing the Siegfried and Maginot Lines, though they are known to be meeting stronger German resistance as they drive through Lorraine for the German frontier.

They hold Pont-a-Mousson, midway between Metz and Nancy.

There was little news, too, of the other American drive towards Germany, through Belgium.

It was confirmed that Namur, on the road to Liege and to Aachen, in Germany, was occupied.

Paris radio said the Allies had occupied Aachen, and Vichy radio reported "fighting on German soil" in this area.

Canadian troops are now on the Channel coast opposite Dover. Their patrols have reached the coast a mile or two east and west of Calais, and are probing the port's defences.

These columns from the Somme have by-passed Boulogne where enemy resistance is still strong.

LE HAVRE SIEGE

Other Allied troops, making good progress north of the Somme, have reached the line Aire-St. Omer, with Polish troops in the outskirts of St. Omer, twenty miles from Calais and twenty-three from Dunkirk.

Le Havre is still being stubbornly defended by the trapped German garrison. In the area between Boulogne and Antwerp are nearly 60,000 Germans whose only escape route is across the Scheldt and thence by a roundabout route to Germany. The Germans are using everything they can find that floats to ferry troops across the Scheldt.

About 30,000 of the troops are effective and the others are merely milling about trying to find a way home, correspondents report.

There was little definite news yesterday of the British thrust into Holland, though unofficial reports said we were "in sight of Rotterdam." General Dempsey's British armour is extending the Allied corridor into Belgium and has now reached the southern outskirts of Ghent, the big inland port of the Scheldt, ten air miles from the Dutch border.

The speed of the British drive to Holland so surprised the Germans that not only did they fail to wreck the Port of Antwerp, but they had no time to flood the country from Antwerp to Maastricht and thus slow up our entry into Holland.

➤ *Daily Mirror* correspondent Rex North, right, and Allied troops enjoy a drink at a French bar near the German border.

"If we're going to fight to the last man we'd better start finding some humans!"

ALLIES ARE SURE OF VICTORY – BERLIN RADIO

"THE Allies are now sure of victory."

This amazing sentence was uttered by Dr. Joseph Saal, German war commentator, in a broadcast to the German people yesterday from Berlin.

He went on to speak mysteriously of various "important factors" which he claimed were in favour of the Germans.

"What they are we do not know in detail," he said, "but the main thing is that they exist and will be incorporated into our strategy in good time.

"Everybody is asking: 'How can we master this situation?' The answer is resistance to the last, defence of the Reich and within its frontiers."

◀ The Germans' situation seemed desperate in August 1944.

HITLER CALLS HIS GENERALS FOR CRISIS TALKS

HITLER has called an urgent meeting of all available army Generals and party chiefs to examine Germany's present military and political situation, according to reports reaching Madrid from Berlin.

The meeting, in Berlin, is to last several days, and the reports state that the position is to be examined "from a realistic viewpoint."

Goering, it is stated, is of opinion that further fighting is futile and hopeless, and he has the firm support of many of the Generals and some of the Nazi leaders.

Ribbentrop and Goebbels are said to be in full agreement that Hitler must make a last attempt at peace, which, if unsuccessful, would justify the use of gas warfare.

▲ An RAF reconnaissance Spitfire photographs the scene in Holland after Allied airborne troops had parachuted in from gliders.

23 September 1944

AIRBORNE IN ARNHEM HELL

FIGHTING FOR THEIR LIVES AS BRITISH 2ND ARMY STRUGGLE TO REACH THEM

BRITISH airborne troops in the Arnhem pocket last night fought for their lives, tantalised by the distant thunder of British Second Army guns and tanks firing at the six miles of Germans wedged between them.

They had been fighting for six days and nights inside the German lines, waiting for Dempsey's men to help them capture the Lek (Rhine) crossing – the last big water barrier to the turning of the Siegfried Line.

"CRITICAL BUT NOT HOPELESS YET" was the way their plight was described at SHAEF last night after a foggy day in which planes could not fly replacements or supplies.

A dramatic message received from Arnhem last night written by Alan Wood yesterday morning said:

It has been a nasty morning – so far cold and mist – and the Germans are plastering us plentifully with mortars, big guns and 88s. The 88s are worst because you don't hear them coming. Machine-guns have just opened up on the right.

In this patch of hell our men are holding a few civilian houses that still stand. An old lady in black stumbled out of one of them a few minutes ago and a British soldier ran out and put his arm round her. She collapsed and he carried her down to safety in a cellar.

It is now just five days and five sleepless nights since we flew out from England. God knows from what secret source of strength these fighting men have drawn the guts which has kept them going.

Only one thing is certain. They will keep going until the Second Army gets here.

◀ British soldiers take a rest after liberating the Dutch town of Nijmegen.

▶ German soldiers bring out their wounded in Holland in September 1944.

ATTACK ON HOLLAND "FINGER" SMASHED

From GEORGE McCARTHY, Daily Mirror Chief Correspondent,
Nijmegen, Thursday

THE vitally important bridge across the River Waal at Nijmegen has been captured intact after a brilliant dual attack by American paratroops and the armoured spearhead of a famous British regiment.

Today British tanks and transport are streaming across the bridge to fight their way forward to link up with the paratroops who, encircled, are holding off the enemy in the region of Arnhem.

The advance to the north continues unchecked. But the Allied commanders in this daring manoeuvre to outflank and cut off a great mass of Germans, are well aware of the risk they run.

They have, in fact, thrust out a lean strong arm straight into enemy territory.

On our left flank, south of Nijmegen, the Germans launched a well-planned attack at Zon and Helmond at eight o'clock today. The battle went on for three hours.

Then, after paratroops and British infantry had brought the enemy to a halt, the roads were cleared and the streams of traffic moved on.

And an hour ago, as I came back to Nijmegen, the Germans opened fire with 88 millimetre guns on the village of St. Oedenrode and I sheltered within the local café until the firing should stop.

One shell landed in the café garden, smashed the brick garage but inflicted no wounds.

And as I emerged the sky was filled with Dakotas flying north to drop more supplies to the paratroops of Arnhem.

Out of the clouds three enemy fighters appeared. There was a burst of machine-gun fire and one Dakota came floating down in flames.

And in Nijmegen itself the people are still cheering, although the Germans are firing across the river, knocking holes in houses and shattering shop fronts.

Before they ran they set fire to many houses by pouring petrol inside them and setting them alight. But with the seizing of the river the battle has been won.

🔺 American tanks pass a windmill in Holland on their way to the front line.

RED ARMY IS AT GATES OF HUNGARY

ADVANCE units of the Red Army, pushing through Rumania, are moving swiftly on the Hungarian border. Before them stretches the open plain to Budapest.

Colonel Ernst von Hammer, the German military commentator, reported last night that Soviet forces had reached Arad on the Maros River in Rumania, only fifteen miles from the Hungarian border.

Moving in high gear on three fronts, the Red Army is advancing swiftly on Hungary, Tallinn (Reval) and Riga, says a Moscow dispatch.

The Poles fighting in Warsaw have established contact with the advanced Soviet troops on the western bank of the Vistula. More arms and ammunition were dropped by British airmen.

➤ A B-26 Marauder bomber attacks the Neuenberg rail bridge across the Rhine as the US Seventh Army drives towards Germany.

SKY-MEN FOUGHT TO FINISH FOR A BRIDGE . . .

The full story of the British airborne troops' eight-day stand in the pocket west of Arnhem against overwhelming odds has yet to be told.

But here is the story, in dramatic detail, of the glorious fight of the handful of British paratroops who tried to hold the bridge at Arnhem for the advancing Second Army, as told by –

GEORGE McCARTHY,
Daily Mirror Chief Correspondent,
Nijmegen, Sunday

DIRTY, unshaven, blood-stained, four paratroopers stumbled up the bank of the Lower Rhine into our lines.

They brought the first story of the fearful seven days in which a small force of paratroopers, isolated even from the glider troops, fought to seize and hold the vital bridge at Arnhem.

Those four men had not only fought for three days and nights when surrounded at the end of the bridge, but, when taken prisoner and removed to Germany, they managed to escape.

One of them, little, lean-faced Lieutenant Dennis Simpson, of the Royal Engineers, of Marborough-road, West Derby, Liverpool, told me the story.

The glider-borne men were further down the river and the paratroopers could not contact. By Wednesday, however, they had battled forward to the bridge itself and held it against an overwhelming enemy opposition.

The Germans themselves wanted that bridge badly. If they could get it they could race men and armour south to the Nijmegen bridge and clear it of our airborne men before the British tanks and infantry could arrive. But the paratroops stopped them.

They charged the pillbox guarding the bridge and set fire to an ammunition dump inside the pillbox, which blew up. Twenty Germans ran out with their hands up.

The enemy brought up his guns and shelled these paratroops out of their positions. Our men took to the cluster of houses, including a schoolhouse, around the approach to the bridge.

The next enemy move was to machine-gun the school from the rooftops of adjoining buildings.

When this failed they set several houses on fire, hoping that the wind would carry the flames to the school. That move failed, too.

In the end all that were left, about forty-five, were driven from the bridge into the last remaining houses and on them the Germans concentrated all their guns.

The battle could not last long. Our men had no ammunition and no food. At the end of half an hour there were thirty-five wounded.

So it was decided to leave four men with the wounded and give the rest a chance to escape.

But as they got clear of the houses the Germans closed in and forced the last six of the gallant band to surrender.

"We were only a handful in those last houses," Simpson said, "and when the Germans forced their way into the outer ones the end seemed to be in sight. In fact, we fought on for days. These Germans mortared and machine-gunned our positions but made little impression."

HELD THEIR FIRE

"Then five German armoured cars and twelve half-tracks appeared from the southern approach of the bridge and rolled across. They fired into the British position as they passed but our troops held their fire until the half-tracks appeared.

"Then a British corporal and private leaned out of a window, one with a Bren gun the other with a Sten.

"They opened fire and within a few seconds every German in the first six half-tracks was either dead or wounded. At the same time fire was opened on the other six and soon every one was blazing and stopped.

"The Germans now brought everything to bear. They mortared and machine-gunned with new violence but in the end they were driven off just as night fell.

"The next day – Plus 3 – was so quiet that we thought the Germans had pulled out, but at 10 o'clock in the morning two Tigers came alongside the quay and started battering away once more.

"By this time we had rigged out a radio and were talking from one house to another comparing notes.

"From our second floor we could see Germans working on the bridge and realised that they were putting in demolition charges.

"It was time for us to take action.

"We rushed out with fixed bayonets through the enemy fire, cleared the enemy away from the bridge and removed the charges. Then the Germans counter-attacked and drove our fellows out.

"We withdrew to our houses, but only for the time being as we organised another bayonet charge.

"This time we suffered heavy casualties, but all the charges were removed.

"By this time the enemy was closing in on us. They set fire to the school. The flames spread and the building began to fall in.

"The Germans returned with three tanks. A British private leaned out of a window and neatly dropped a bomb on one of them. It blew up. But the paratroopers' position was desperate.

"A group of their comrades cut off and besieged in a group of houses along the road signalled that they withdraw from the approach to the bridge. It was decided to counter-attack."

BAYONET CHARGE

"So the paratroop men with bayonets fixed emerged from their houses, charged down the road and reached the safety of a house where the last stand was made."

The rest of the glowing story was told by Corporal Charles Weir, of Richmond-terrace, Aberdeen, and Corporal John Humphreys, of Wormsley, Herefordshire, as they munched food at an open-air kitchen.

Weir told how they were confined in a building when captured by the Germans. They saw a chance of escape and took it.

It was just another adventure for Humphreys. He had already been captured in the Italian campaign. He escaped from prison at Ancona.

"But it was a tough do on the bridge at Arnhem," Humphreys admitted between hungry bites into a huge meat sandwich. . . . "A tough do."

◗ The airborne assault on Arnhem is captured in Philip Zec's cartoon.

The Landing

28 September 1944

1 IN 4 RESCUED FROM HELL OF ARNHEM

ABOUT 2,000 of the 8,000 British airborne troops who made the epic eight-day stand in the blazing hell of the Arnhem pocket have been evacuated, it was announced at SHAEF at midnight.

Some 1,200 wounded could not be withdrawn to the south bank of the Lower Rhine. Reports indicate that the Germans are treating them well.

Some of the Polish airborne reinforcements and British Second Army infantrymen who crossed to the north bank have also been saved.

The survivors of the first bid to win a crossing over the last big water barrier to the North German plain are being given every possible comfort in rest areas behind the battle lines.

Victory cost the enemy dear. Between 12,000 and 15,000 Germans were killed, according to an unofficial Allied estimate.

The "red devils'" sacrifice was not in vain. Without it the British Second Army could not have hoped to capture the even more vital Nijmegen bridge.

A British soldier evacuated from Arnhem arrives in Nijmegen minus some of his clothes.

THEY CALLED THE CHEEKY PULL-OUT 'OPERATION BERLIN'

From ALAN WOOD, with Arnhem Airborne Force,
Tuesday (delayed)

THIS is the end. The most tragic and glorious battle of the war is over, and the survivors of this British airborne force can sleep soundly for the first time in eight days and nights.

Orders came to us yesterday to break out from our forest citadel west of Arnhem, cross the Rhine and join up with the Second Army on the south bank.

Our commander decided against a concerted assault on the Germans round us.

Instead, the plan was to split up into little groups, ten to twenty strong, setting out along different routes at two-minute intervals, which would simply walk through the German lines in the dark.

Cheeky patrols went out earlier tying bits of white parachute tape to trees to mark the way.

To hinder the Germans waking up to what was happening, Second Army guns laid down a battering box barrage all the afternoon.

The first party was to set off at 10 p.m.; our group was to leave at 10.04 p.m.

They went round distributing little packets of sulphanilamide and morphia. We tore up blankets and strapped them round our boots to muffle the sound of our feet in the trees.

We were told the password – "John Bull."

If we became separated, each man was to make his way by compass due south until he reached the river.

Our major is an old hand. He led the way, and linked our party together by getting everyone to hold the tail of the parachutist's smock of the man in front of him, so our infiltrating column had an absurd resemblance to some children's game.

It was half-light, with the glow of fires from burning houses around, when we set out.

We were lucky; we went through a reputed enemy pocket without hearing a shot, except for a stray sniper's bullet.

Another group met a machine-gun with a fixed line of fire across their path. Another had to silence a bunch of Germans with a burst of Sten fire and hand grenades. Another had to pause while a German finished his evening stroll across their pathway.

But we all got through without the enemy realising that we were doing anything more than normal night patrolling.

The worst part was waiting two hours by the riverside till our turn came for assault boats to ferry us across.

The Germans, if not yet definitely suspicious, were inquisitive; they kept on sending up flares, and it was vital to lie flat and motionless.

In our boat queue we lay flat and shivering on a soaking field with cold rain drizzling down. Occasionally machine-guns spattered out and bullets tweaked through the grass.

We were lucky again: our actual crossing was quiet. But soon after it seemed that the Germans had guessed what was going on, because they mortared and shelled heavily along the shallow river banks.

One soldier in the next field was hit and called out for help.

Men whose turn for a place in the boats had come after hours

of waiting insisted on staying under fire a little longer so that the wounded could go first.

Any wounded left behind, of course, become automatically prisoners of war; so many sick and limping left their beds to take a chance with the escape parties.

And so this epic stand of the British airborne soldiers ended as it had been fought – with honour, with high courage, with selfless sacrifice.

What of the spirit of these men as they trudged back through the wet night to the billets where they are now sunk in sodden sleep?

You can best judge it by the name they chose for last night's break out. It had the same objective as they have always had, and they still mean to get in there. They called it "Operation Berlin."

'I PRAYED TO SEE HACKNEY WICK AGAIN'

WORST ordeals of the nightmare siege at Arnhem were attacks by flame-throwers, which seared the airborne out of trenches and houses, according to 30-year-old Lance-Corporal John Stillwell, of Ballance-road, Hackney Wick, one of the men who came back.

"I prayed to God I would live to see Hackney Wick again – and I never believed I should," said Stillwell, wrapped up in an Army blanket.

"We had twenty civilians with us in a house. They were in the cellars. When we left they cried to us: 'Please don't leave us.'

"But we had to. We made our way down to the river through another lane of withering fire.

"One man, wounded in the leg, kept three Vickers guns going all alone to hold the escape channel open."

Said one "red devil" officer, Captain Bethune Taylor, of Landsdowne place, Cheltenham, "I was in Crete, and that was a piece of cake compared with Arnhem."

And last night the *Daily Mirror* brought fifty-seven-year-old Mrs. M. Stillwell the first news of her son since he was last on leave weeks ago.

"Thank God," she exclaimed. "I've been so worried about him, and I guessed he was in this business." She broke down and cried.

➤ Firemen, members of the Home Guard, the Air Raid Precaution wardens and civilians search the wreckage of bomb-damaged houses in Leytonstone, north-east London, after a V1 bomb attack.

An RAF Halifax bomber flies over a German synthetic oil plant during a daylight attack in October 1944.

CHURCHILL GOES TO SEE STALIN

MR. CHURCHILL, and Mr. Eden, the Foreign Secretary, arrived in Moscow yesterday.

This was announced in Parliament by Mr. Attlee after Moscow had broadcast the news.

Mr. Attlee said the Premier and Mr. Eden had gone to Moscow "for discussions with Marshal Stalin and M. Molotov."

The meeting, he said, is a sequel to the Quebec Conference. It has the "fullest approval" of the U.S. Government, and the U.S. Ambassador in Moscow, Mr. Harriman, will represent the U.S. Government.

With the Premier and Foreign Secretary are Field Marshal Sir Alan Brooke, Chief of the Imperial General Staff, and General Sir Hastings Ismay, Chief of Staff to the Minister of Defence.

This is Mr. Churchill's second visit to Moscow – he was there the last time in 1942 – and it will be his third meeting with Marshal Stalin. The last was at Teheran in November, 1943.

THE CAREER MONTY WRECKED IS NOW ENDED: ROMMEL IS DEAD

FIELD-MARSHAL ROMMEL was "written off" by the unknown Allied fighter-bomber pilot who shot up a German staff car in France in July.

This was revealed last night when the German News Agency announced Rommel's death "as the result of a car accident received when C.-in-C. of an Army Group in the West."

The "accident" was the swoop of one of our pilots.

Rommel, fanatical follower of Hitler and built up by the Nazi Party into a great "victory" general, won his fame by dashing victories in Libya. His career hit a sudden slump when he met Alexander and Montgomery.

Not long after Rommel had been brought to Berlin to tell the neutral Press that his Afrika Korps had Egypt in its grip, his army was pulverised at Alamein.

And when D-Day came, Rommel found himself again facing his great rival – Montgomery.

It is not known how far Rommel was responsible for the tactics which gave the British general his chance to turn the Battle of Normandy into the annihilation of the German Seventh Army.

Rommel had his "car accident" just before Montgomery's colossal right hook started moving at St. Lo.

Hitler has ordered a State funeral.

IT MADE D-DAY SEEM A PICNIC BUT WE LANDED

At the assault on Westkapelle was Arthur Oakeshott, Reuter's special correspondent, who gives this description of the battle.

IT is difficult to say how our men did it, but they did.

The veterans said D-Day was a picnic by comparison; that it was far worse than the Dieppe raid; but Westkapelle is ours now, and how our boys did it is one of the epics of this or any other war.

Losses in the ratio of four out of five were suffered by the close support craft. Nevertheless, the operation was a complete success.

It was originally planned that the RAF should give the area a forty-eight hours' concentrated bombing "softener" immediately prior to the attack.

Weather, however, made this impossible, and the Royal Marine Commandos in the "little ships" of the Royal Navy had to go in facing the worst shellfire of the war.

In the first few minutes, as I watched from my landing craft, close inshore, ship after ship burst into flames and disappeared in a pall of thick smoke and flame, or blew to pieces with a terrific crumbling roar, or again yawed about helplessly, engines smashed, steering gear gone and the crew and cargo of Commandos, tanks and equipment virtually annihilated.

400-MILE WESTERN FRONT IS ABLAZE

"IKE" ATTACKS WITH SIX ARMIES

SIX Allied armies – more than General Eisenhower has ever sent into action at one time before – are now attacking along the 400-mile front from Arnhem to the Swiss border.

Three of those armies are battling on a front perhaps only seventy-five miles long menacing Cologne and the industrial

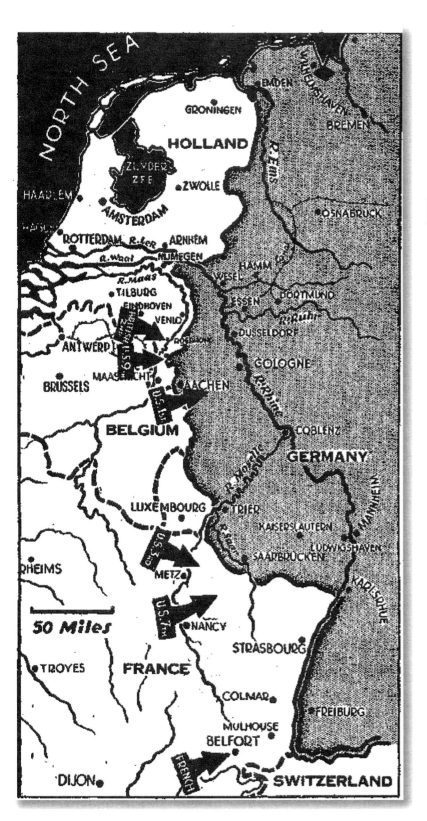

Rhineland. Here a "secret" army, shuffled about for months to deceive the enemy, has joined the British Second and U.S. First Armies.

A new First Army attack beyond Aachen was spearheaded yesterday by 1,150 Lancasters and Halifaxes, escorted by 250 Mustangs and Spitfires, and 1,200 U.S. heavies with 450 escorting fighters.

They put down a barrage of at least 8,000 tons of bombs in a great arc twenty miles ahead of Aachen.

23 November 1944

BOMBED, THEY HELPED NEIGHBOUR

FAMILIES had settled down for the evening, with the children in bed, when a bomb fell in a street in a working-class district of Southern England recently.

One row of little houses received a direct hit. Some were brought to the ground, and others were shattered by the blast.

But within a short time the street was working together to rescue the families in the ruins of their homes.

Before rescue services arrived families had dug themselves out and were helping to bring out their neighbours and their children.

Mr. Lilley was in the basement of his house with his wife and two daughters when the bomb fell.

"Everything collapsed on us," he said, "and in the darkness I could hear my daughters scream but I could not see them. I dug myself out, and then managed to clear away the rubble from the others. We are all unhurt."

Mrs. Hill was at home with her two children, aged 8 and 13. The house collapsed about them, and Mrs. Hill was killed, but the two children were brought out alive.

All the residents of the street helped each other to account for their missing members and to salvage their belongings.

Two dead have so far been recovered, but others are still missing.

P.G. WODEHOUSE RELEASE HELD UP BY PARIS POLICE

P.G. WODEHOUSE, the novelist, who was arrested in Paris by the French police on charges of aiding the Germans by his broadcasts from Berlin in 1941, was still in gaol late last night despite reports that he had been released conditionally.

The condition was that he and his wife, who was arrested with him, should get out of Paris within eight days to any place at least sixty miles from the capital, and that he should be under police surveillance. It was reported in London that the charges had been dropped.

But a Reuter message just before midnight said Wodehouse was still being held at the headquarters of the Paris C.I.D. The French police refused either to confirm or deny the reported decision to release him – a report given confirmation by an official of the British Foreign Office.

The novelist was spending a third night in prison.

An Associated Press dispatch from Paris said it was understood that the British Government had investigated the question of Wodehouse's radio speeches from Germany, and had given him a "clean bill of health" three weeks ago.

This message also said that the SHAEF censors, for some reason unknown, stopped the news of arrest for several hours.

Officials were unable to explain in what way security was involved in the Wodehouse affair, particularly since Paris is now under French Civil administration. The British Embassy in Paris was stated to be negotiating in the case. In London, the Foreign Office, M.I.5 (Intelligence), and Home Office discussed the situation.

"The position at the moment is a poser," said a Foreign Office spokesman during the evening.

◗ British troops trudge through deep mud in Holland in December 1944.

F.D.R. TELLS AMERICA BRITAIN MADE THE INVASION POSSIBLE

IF Britain had not been supplying the 2,000,000 American soldiers and airmen who came here for the invasion, it would have taken 1,000 ships to bring their stuff across the Atlantic.

Without Britain's all-out sacrifices there would have been no Second Front this summer. This is "reverse lease-lend," on which President Roosevelt has reported to Congress.

The thousand ships we saved brought 6,800,000 tons of tanks, lorries, guns, bombs and other war material.

In the six months they were hotting up the invasion Britain provided the Americans with 3,851,000 ship tons of supplies.

Reverse lease-lend from us to America – a more graphic phrase than "mutual aid," the label they use now – which does not tell the world that Britain is paying back – has cost us 3,348 million dollars.

At four to the pound that is £837millions, and the figure comes to life when it is mentioned that Britain's 1938–39 revenue, in Sir John Simon's 1939 Budget, was only £927millions.

WE FED THEM

We provided the U.S. Forces over here (says President Roosevelt) with 63 per cent, of their eatables, and so on, and 58 per cent, of their engineer supplies. In cold figures the President sees the great benefit the U.S.A. has received from reverse lease-lend.

But in the larger sense of a contribution towards victory, the benefit the U.S.A. has received from Britain is far larger, he says.

But neither Britain nor the U.S.A. is counting its contributions as so much cash.

"There is no statistical or money measurements for the value of courage, skill and sacrifice in the face of death and destruction wrought by our common enemies," observes President Roosevelt.

BRITAIN HELPS ALL THE OTHERS

A table of the help that Britain has given "with compliments, no charge," to other warrior nations up to last June:

U.S.A £604,730,000
Russia 269,457,000
France 13,600,000
China 9,050,000
Poland 120,000,000
Czechoslovakia 18,629,000
Greece 12,368,000
Turkey 20,681,000
Portugal 11,133,000
[Total] 1,079,648,000
Russia has had 51,000 British aircraft and 24,700 tanks and trucks.

20 December 1944

LEAVE BALLOT: W.O. SENDING WIVES WIRES

From HILDE MARCHANT,
Dutch Frontier, Tuesday

FIRST Army leave ballots took place on the Western Front today. Special dispatch riders took the news to lucky men in the field. First men to go will be D-Day troops.

Lists will shortly be flown over from Holland and Belgium, and the War Office will then send telegrams telling relatives when to expect their men.

Many of the men are returning in January – the first leave month – to marry girls who have waited years for them.

One of these happy men is Corporal George Kettle, of Grantham, who drew January 10 out of the lucky dip in the Lincolnshire Regiment ballot.

George landed on D-Day and has been in forward front line positions practically ever since. He told me he is going back to Devon to marry Miss Dorothy Collard, of 12, St, Andrew's-street, Tiverton. Other lucky men told me they go back to England to see children they have never seen.

The system of ballot is generally accepted as good by the troops. Each unit is given allocation and the names of men first eligible drawn out of the hat.

2 January 1945

CROWDS' ROAR WELCOMED THE LEAVE BOYS BACK TO LONDON

CHEERING crowds roared a welcome to the first batch of seven-day leave men from the Western Front when they arrived in two trains at a London terminus last night.

As the soldiers poured off the trains under the glare of arc lights, wives and children, parents and sweethearts, pressed against the barriers, flushed, excited – and some of them in tears.

The men walked along a lane through the cheering folk to board special buses and trains which were to take them to homes in London and all parts of the country.

And as they struggled through into the moonlit London streets, they were showered with cigarettes and sweets and kisses. In their ears were ringing the welcome of the cheering thousands: "Happy New Year, boys! You've done a grand job!"

◗ Private Robert Martin from Glasgow is welcomed home on leave at Waverley station, Edinburgh, in January 1945.

Germany's Last Stand

An increasingly desperate Hitler was determined to mount one final offensive. He had already survived an attack on his life by a disenchanted German general and many Nazi officers wanted to throw in the towel. But shortly before Christmas 1944 he gave the order to attack in the Ardennes. It took the Allies completely by surprise and soon there was a "Bulge" in the Western Front, caused by a concentrated German advance west towards Antwerp. The Allies were outnumbered and their losses were heavy. Around 19,000 Americans lost their lives. The German dead approached 100,000. It proved an all or nothing attack.

◀ British troops on patrol in snow gear during the wintry and bloody Battle of the Bulge in Belgium in January 1945.

147

DAILY MIRROR, Monday, December 18, 1944.

Daily Mirror

No. 12,793
ONE PENNY

DEC 18

Registered at the G.P.O. as a Newspaper.

Rundstedt throws in skytroops, tanks, planes

MAJOR GERMAN ATTACK: AMERICAN LINE HOLED

"Russia has no liberation worries"

What amounts to a comment on Allied policy towards the people of liberated countries, came from Ilya Ehrenburg in the Russian newspaper "Pravda" yesterday.

"The democracies," he said, "cannot liberate a people from Fascism of one kind while at the same time handing them over to Fascism of another kind."

Ehrenburg made the pointed comment that "the Red Army knows how to liberate — witness the freed Poles, Norwegians, Serbs and Slovaks."

"No Semi-Fascists"

"When we of the Red Army liberate a people we do not replace Fascists with semi-Fascists," he said.

"It must be remembered that the peoples of Europe have fought gallantly against traitors, and those who did the fighting cannot be packed off like paid servants when they have done their duty."

DON'T UNDERRATE THIS PUNCH, SAYS DAVID WALKER

U.S. FIRST ARMY, Sunday.

THIS is the greatest German counter-attack since the Allies landed on the Continent.

The battle on our front is being fought in grey but fairly clear weather, with aircraft up in strength against the usual background of V-weapons which have been streaming over this part of the country on an increased scale.

Up to a late hour yesterday it appeared to be a series of small-scale counter-attacks.

Today we are involved in a large-scale battle which may well affect the future conduct of the war in the West.

It would be idiotic to underrate the strength of this enemy punch, which has been deliberately made on his own initiative and despite the probability of serious losses in manpower and material.

"Your great hour has struck. Everything is at stake. Give your all in one last effort."—German Field-Marshal von Rundstedt's Order of the Day to his troops.

THE Germans have begun a full-scale counter-offensive on the Western Front comparable to their breakthrough bid in March, 1918.

Spearheaded by paratroops dropped miles ahead and backed by strong forces of planes and tanks, they have broken through the American lines in many places on a seventy-mile front in the wooded Ardennes Hills.

Fighting is raging inside once-liberated Belgium and Luxembourg a few miles behind the lines held three days ago by the U.S. First Army.

Last night the Huns had advanced some miles and driven wedges to within eight miles of Malmedy, important Belgian road and rail hub, and eighteen miles of the city of Luxembourg.

Many penetrations have, however, been sealed off.

The Luftwaffe is up in strength, and big air battles raged over the battlefront.

One Allied air force, flying more than 1,000 sorties, knocked 110 out of 250 German fighters and bombers out of the sky for the loss of thirty-five.

The counter-offensive began on Saturday morning, with a dozen light punches launched against the First Army's southern sector.

These attacks were the feelers for the real weight which was thrown in at dawn yesterday, cables Edward Connolly, Exchange war correspondent.

Then the enemy thrust reached the scale of a major counter-attack, rapidly rising to the weight of what SHAEF at midnight called a full-scale counter-offensive.

Before a heavy artillery barrage put it in gear, scores of German paratroops, floating below their black parachutes, were dropped inside Belgium, south-east of Aachen, at points several miles behind the American lines.

Divisions Sent In

The paratroopers' job was to cut roads to prevent Allied reinforcements being rushed up.

The first enemy sky troops were dropped at 3.45 a.m. Many of them have since been rounded up.

But pitched battles are still raging inside woods and at road junctions against groups of paratroops.

Whole divisions were flung into battle. At one point enemy infantry divisions were supported by elements of panzer divisions.

These are but part of the great strength arrayed against us, and the number of tanks spearheading these forces is unprecedented for this campaign.

I was told at forward H.Q. that this is the Germans'

last throw of the dice, an all-out breakthrough bid.

Any doubts on that score are removed by two significant sidelights.

One is the capture of an order of the day issued by Rundstedt, the German commander, which declared: "Now is the time for the German Army to strike."

The other evidence lies in the strength of the panzers and planes opposing the Americans. They include forces which have long been stored biding their time for the major attack.

According to a Reuter message from SHAEF the German High Command is apparently ready to keep up its attacks for some time.

Meanwhile, SHAEF has drawn a security screen over the U.S. Seventh Army, now hurling itself against the section of the Siegfried Line guarding the corridor along the west bank of the Rhine

General Eisenhower, the Supreme Commander, was in a serious mood when outlining war developments to U.S. Congressmen who visited his advance command post recently.

Greece: "Bulgar invasion" mystery

REPORTS coming from Greek Government sources in Athens last night said that several hundreds of Bulgarians had crossed the frontier into Northern Greece.

The reports said the Bulgarians were believed to be armed, but it was not known whether they were deserters from the Bulgarian Army or guerrillas.

It is suggested they may be taking advantage of the Greek civil war to seize Greek territory, although it is added that the Bulgarian Government is not implicated.

Shelling was resumed in Athens late yesterday after more than twenty-four hours of comparative quiet and fighting is continuing around Omonia Square.

Spitfires strafed the stadium area as well as a concentration of ELAS forces on the outskirts of Athens.

Rocket-firing Beaufighters have been used to attack ELAS headquarters in the northern part of Athens, it became known last night.

Another target for these planes was an ELAS-held railway line, on which an engine was blown up.

EAM has not yet replied to General Scobie's renewed demand that the ELAS forces in Attica should be disarmed.

All Greek reserve officers between the ages of 25 and 31 living in Athens, the Piraeus and suburbs were ordered to report for active service yesterday in the most extensive call-up ordered by the Greek Government since the outbreak of the fighting.

General Plastiras, the "strong man" who pulled Greece together after the disastrous war with Turkey in 1922, broadcast an appeal to ELAS last night to lay down their arms.

He flew to Greece from the South of France a few days ago at the urgent request of the Greek Premier.

Right wing elements in Athens, fearful of the plan for a Regency as a concession to the Left, have sent telegrams to King George urging him to oppose it.

THREE DIE IN OCTU CAMP BLAZE

Three officer-cadets died early yesterday in a dormitory fire at an OCTU camp at Alton (Staffs). Two of eight others who escaped by plunging through the dormitory windows when they woke to find the place ablaze are in hospital with injuries and burns.

The dead are: Officer-Cadet W. G. Burwell, 28, married; Officer-Cadet E. Forster, 19, single; and Officer-Cadet T. C. Malone, 27, married.

"LEGION OF THE DOOMED WILL PILOT THE V4"

LATEST secret weapon "horror story"—published yesterday in Stockholm—says that several hundred incurable German war invalids have volunteered to fly the newest German V weapon, V4, to London.

It will be a one-way journey for them, with death at its inevitable end, for V4 is a suicide bomb, controlled by a pilot throughout its flight until the moment it crashes, states the Free German Press Bureau.

Pilots are now being trained, both technically and "psychologically," in special schools near the German Baltic coast say the Germans.

BONOMI'S DENIAL

Signor Bonomi yesterday denied a report that he had written a letter to President Roosevelt, giving details of his complaints against Britain

95 Italians tunnel out of British camp

NINETY-FIVE Italians escaped from a prisoner-of-war camp, reputed to accommodate only Fascist prisoners, in Scotland during the week-end.

Forty-seven had been recaptured by late last night, four within seven miles of Glasgow.

Military authorities refused to make any official statement but it is understood the prisoners, many of them said to be of a truculent type, escaped by tunnelling.

The camp is at Doonfoot, near Ayr, and the prisoners apparently crept through the tunnel before dawn on Saturday.

Mother and child are killed by V-bomb

MRS. COLLINS was putting her young daughter Anne, to bed recently when a V-bomb fell just behind the house and buried them under the wreckage. Rescuers working by the aid of searchlights brought out the mother and child dead.

There was one other death—a passenger in one of two buses which were crossing a bridge nearby. Other passengers were injured.

A printing works was damaged and a number of houses wrecked.

One woman, tattered but unhurt, was led from the scene, moaning, "I saw my baby move. . . Oh, God, I saw him move."

Mr. William Church stood outside his broken house, while rescue workers dug feverishly for his mother and father, sister and sister's fiance, who were buried in a collapsed front room. "One day," he said thickly, "we shall repay this."

Picture of a V-bomb incident in Back Page.

LANCASTERS BOMB DANUBE RAIL TOWN

Lancasters flew to the Danube last night to make the first major attack on the industrial and rail town of Ulm, on the left bank of the river between Stuttgart and Munich.

Bombers were heard streaming over one S.E. Coast district for an hour.

18 December 1944

RUNDSTEDT THROWS IN SKYTROOPS, TANKS, PLANES

MAJOR GERMAN ATTACK: AMERICAN LINE HOLED

"Your great hour has struck. Everything is at stake. Give your all in one last effort."

– German Field-Marshal von Rundstedt's
Order of the Day to his troops

THE Germans have begun a full-scale counter-offensive on the Western Front comparable to their breakthrough bid in March, 1918.

Spearheaded by paratroops dropped miles ahead and backed by strong forces of planes and tanks, they have broken through the American lines in many places on a seventy-mile front in the wooded Ardennes Hills.

Fighting is raging inside once-liberated Belgium and Luxembourg a few miles behind the lines held three days ago by the U.S. First Army.

Last night the Huns had advanced some miles and driven wedges to within eight miles of Malmedy, important Belgian road and rail hub, and eighteen miles of the city of Luxembourg.

Many penetrations have, however, been sealed off.

The Luftwaffe is up in strength, and big air battles raged over the battlefront.

One Allied air force, flying more than 1,000 sorties, knocked 110 out of 250 German fighters and bombers out of the sky for the loss of thirty-five.

The counter-offensive began on Saturday morning, with a dozen light punches launched against the First Army's southern sector.

These attacks were the feelers for the real weight which was thrown in at dawn yesterday, cables Edward Connolly, Exchange war correspondent.

Then the enemy thrust reached the scale of a major counter-attack, rapidly rising to the weight of what SHAEF at midnight called a full-scale counter-offensive.

Before a heavy artillery barrage put it in gear, scores of German paratroops, floating below their black parachutes, were dropped inside Belgium, south-east of Aachen, at points several miles behind the American lines.

DIVISIONS SENT IN

The paratroopers' job was to cut roads to prevent Allied reinforcements being rushed up.

The first enemy sky troops were dropped at 3.45 a.m. Many of them have since been rounded up.

But pitched battles are still raging inside woods and at road junctions against groups of paratroops.

Whole divisions were flung into battle. At one point enemy infantry divisions were supported by elements of panzer divisions.

They are but part of the great strength arrayed against us and the number of tanks spearheading these forces is unprecedented for this campaign.

I was told at forward H.Q. that this is the Germans' last throw of the dice, an all-out breakthrough bid.

Any doubts on that score are removed by two significant sidelights. One is the capture of an order of the day issued by Rundstedt, the German commander, which declared: "Now is the time for the German Army to strike."

The other evidence lies in the strength of the panzers and planes opposing the Americans. They include forces which have long been stored biding their time for the major attack.

According to a Reuter message from SHAEF, the German High Command is apparently ready to keep up its attacks for some time.

Meanwhile, SHAEF has drawn a security screen over the U.S. Seventh Army, now hurling itself against the section of the Siegfried Line guarding the corridor along the west bank of the Rhine.

DON'T UNDERRATE THIS PUNCH,

Says DAVID WALKER, U.S. First Army, Sunday

THIS is the greatest German counter-attack since the Allies landed on the Continent.

The battle on our front is being fought, in grey but fairly clear weather, with aircraft up in strength against the usual background of V-weapons which have been streaming over this part of the country on an increased scale.

Up to a late hour yesterday it appeared to be a series of small-scale counter-attacks.

Today we are involved in a large-scale battle which may well affect the future conduct of the war in the West.

It would be idiotic to underrate the strength of this enemy punch, which has been deliberately made on his own initiative and despite the probability of serious losses in manpower and material.

DAILY MIRROR, Tuesday, December 19, 1944.

Daily Mirror

DEC 19

No. 12,794
ONE PENNY
Registered
at the G.P.O.
as
a Newspaper.

+ + +

'SUBSTANTIAL GAINS' BY HUNS IN BELGIUM

LIGHTNING BRITISH THRUST RE-OPENS ROAD FROM ATHENS TO THE SEA

BRITISH troops have re-opened the road between Athens and the port of Piræus in a lightning offensive which began before dawn yesterday.

Striking out from both their "island" in the centre of Athens and from their positions in the port of the Piræus, the British troops met little opposition.

Within a few hours the ELAS troops had been cleared from their positions dominating the road between Athens and the port, and shortly afterwards the last ELAS-held stretch of the road was cleared.

This means that the British "island" in the centre of the city, which has been besieged by ELAS troops for several days, has been relieved and that men and supplies will be able to flow in once again.

Tanks in Use

The ELAS stronghold at the Marble Stadium now lies beneath our guns and British paratroops, who have been partially isolated on the top of the Acropolis Hill for ten days, have broken out.

Tanks, armoured cars, smoke bombs and Beaufighters were used in the attack, which followed a night of fierce fighting, during which Athens was lit up by flares and the crackle of machine guns.

Meantime on the political

NO CHARGE AS COUNSEL WAS LOST

Because prosecuting counsel could not be found at Reading yesterday, Private Bernard Jones, 23, of the RASC, was found not guilty on three driving charges at the direction of the Recorder and was bound over on another.

front, although the Archbishop Damaskinos of Athens has consented to become Regent of Greece there has been an eleventh-hour split in the Papandreou Cabinet.

British military circles said yesterday that the purpose of the new offensive is to "raise the siege on the centre of Athens by securing lines of communication with the base at Phaleron Bay and securing direct lines with the Piræus."

The commander of a strong concentration of ELAS forces in the Volos area—120 miles north of Athens—has presented to the commander of the Allied relief units and a small Indian garrison an ultimatum to quit the town, cabled a correspondent last night.

Marguerite Demanges (in uniform), 22, and Henriette Durand, 19, of the French resistance movement, are in London this week as the guests of the Air Ministry and the RAF. See story below.

AMERICAN reinforcements were brought up in Belgium and Luxemburg yesterday as the Germans made what Allied front-line correspondents called "substantial gains" on their seventy-mile wide offensive front.

At least a dozen penetrations of the Allied lines have been made, said a front line report quoted in New York. But the Americans still hold Monschau.

"Measures to deal with the situation are in hand," it was stated at Allied Supreme H.Q.

The German High Command, in its first official announcement of the offensive, said it was launched by "strong German forces, after a short but tremendous artillery preparation."

After over-running forward American positions, the "great offensive, supported by strong fighter formations, is taking a favourable course," the German communique said, claiming the Allies had been taken completely by surprise.

American broadcaster Richard Hottelot, calling from the First U.S. Army sector yesterday, said that the German counter-offensive was still in progress and that more German infantry and tanks had been thrown in.

German tanks had made penetrations "a number of miles deep" in the Allied fronts.

"This morning," Hottelot said, "the enemy poured more material into the battle after a pause of about twelve hours.

"The entire front south of Monschau is in motion. On our side counter measures have been taken.

"The weight of the enemy's tanks has given him a penetration of a number of miles deep into our front. When I left it two hours ago, the situation was still fluid."

"There is no doubt that the threat is a major one," Hottelot added. "It involves crack divisions and material.

Threat to Entire Front

"It is intended to be a serious threat to our entire front. The enemy has more divisions right behind the front line with which to follow up his gains. He must have strained his operational reserves to the utmost.

"The Germans intend to break the back of our winter offensive with this stroke."

Parachutists, captured by the First and Ninth Armies, have revealed that they were formed into special combat-teams for this job more than four weeks ago.

Though the Ninth has cleared up most of the few enemy parachutists in its sector, the First Army still has a number to deal with.

With the Luftwaffe's attacks in support of the ground forces continuing and spreading to the British sector in the north, enemy air losses are mounting. Figures of German planes destroyed in the first day, when they flew over 1,000 sorties, are

Fears big New Year cut in beer

WARNING that drastic beer rationing may be necessary in the New Year was given by Mr. F. A. Simonds, chairman of H. and G. Simonds, Ltd., brewers, of Reading, at the company's annual meeting.

"We are faced in the trade with a grave crisis owing to the shortage of malt stocks," Mr. Simonds said, "and if steps are not taken to ensure a supply of labour for the manufacturers of malt some rationing scheme will be necessary.

"We believe that the Government is at last, after months of forceful representation, realising the seriousness of the cry of 'No beer which will surely arise in the summer and autumn if some relief is not forthcoming."

Mr. Simonds said that they had been sending to the troops abroad many thousands of dozens of bottled beer monthly and an embargo has been placed on all beer exports other than direct to H.M. Forces or the Merchant Navy.

Shot man "ignored police challenge"

Thomas Loughran, nineteen-year-old labourer, of Cinnamond-street, Belfast, was yesterday admitted to a Belfast hospital in a serious condition with a bullet wound in the stomach.

It is understood that shots were fired when two men failed to respond to a police challenge in Divis-street, near the centre of the city.

ORANGES S O S "TO SAVE LITTLE GIRL'S LIFE"

An urgent telephone message received in a RAF station in the north-west at midnight ran: "Can you spare an orange to save the life of a little girl?"

Although a small ration of oranges issued at the station recently had been taken or sent home by the airmen, several oranges were soon forthcoming, and were sent by road to the Fazakerley Isolation Hospital, near Liverpool, where a little girl lay seriously ill.

One-girl 'underground' was eyes and ears of RAF

By Your Special Correspondent

TWO of France's "One-Woman Revolutions" are in London for their first rest-and-enjoyment for four years.

Marguerite had three Resistance chiefs snatched almost out of her hand by the Germans, and still carried on alone, spying, fighting, organising. Now she's sight-seeing.

Henriette, a lush dark damsel, befurred and bejewelled, who was fourteen and a half years old when France fell—and the leader of one of the youngest Resistance groups of all, the pupils of the Champs de Commerce School in Paris, is shop-gazing—she wants a pair of British shoes.

Marguerite was never arrested, but Henriette was rounded-up by what she calls a "barrage of police" at the St. Lazare Station in Paris.

Unfortunately she had her handbag filled with RAF leaflets. Fortunately, she was not the fool the Germans assume any other nationality must be.

She "sold" them the idea that she was much too young and foolish to bother her head about politics, so they didn't bother to imprison her.

Instead, she was sent to work at an aircraft factory.

APPEAL DISMISSED

Appeal of George Frederick Fenton, miner, of North Carlton, near Worksop, against his conviction at Notts Assizes last month on a charge of murdering his landlady Mrs. Mary Elizabeth Wright, was dismissed in the Court of Criminal Appeal yesterday. A woman barrister, Mrs. E. K. Lane, appeared for Fenton.

She learned a lot of things there that were useful to the Allies later on.

Marguerite's work never achieved the Scarlet Pimpernel glamour of her young friend, but it would be difficult to assess the exact value of her four years' fight.

At seventeen she left school and set up on her own, listening to the B.B.C., typing and duplicating the instructions, and peddling them round Viroflay, her home town near Versailles, on her bicycle.

Just Found Out

That was only the beginning. The rest of her career underground makes Mata Hari look as if she weren't trying.

The RAF wanted to know about German Ack Ack positions—Marguerite, still on her bike, found out. They wanted to know what type of aircraft—and how many—the Renault works produced. On Marguerite's information they planned the big daylight raid.

Villacoublay airfield interested the Air Force, though.

Continued on Back Page

BASIL DEAN GOES EAST

Mr. Basil Dean, director of ENSA, has left for India and Burma via the Middle East to examine and develop the entertainment provision generally in these commands.

Continued on Back Page

"RUSSIA HAS NO LIBERATION WORRIES"

What amounts to a comment on Allied policy towards the people of liberated countries, came from Ilya Ehrenburg in the Russian newspaper "Pravda" yesterday.

"The democracies," he said, "cannot liberate a people from Fascism of one kind while at the same time handing them over to Fascism of another kind."

Ehrenburg made the pointed comment that "the Red Army knows how to liberate – witness the freed Poles, Norwegians, Serbs and Slovaks."

"NO SEMI-FASCISTS"

"When we of the Red Army liberate a people we do not replace Fascists with semi-Fascists," he said.

"It must be remembered that the peoples of Europe have fought gallantly against traitors, and those who did the fighting cannot be packed off like paid servants when they have done their duty."

19 December 1944

'SUBSTANTIAL GAINS' BY HUNS IN BELGIUM

AMERICAN reinforcements were brought up in Belgium and Luxembourg yesterday as the Germans made what Allied front-line correspondents called "substantial gains" on their seventy-mile wide offensive front.

At least a dozen penetrations of the Allied lines have been made, said a front line report quoted in New York. But the Americans still hold Monschau.

"Measures to deal with the situation are in hand," it was stated at Allied Supreme H.Q.

The German High Command, in its first official announcement of the offensive, said it was launched by "strong German forces, after a short but tremendous artillery preparation."

After over-running forward American positions, the "great offensive, supported by strong fighter formations, is taking a favourable course," the German communiqué said, claiming the Allies had been taken completely by surprise.

American broadcaster Richard Hottelot, calling from the First U.S. Army sector yesterday, said that the German counter-offensive was still in progress and that more German infantry and tanks had been thrown in.

German tanks had made penetrations "a number of miles deep" in the Allied fronts.

"This morning," Hottelot said, "the enemy poured more material into the battle after a pause of about twelve hours.

"The entire front south of Monschau is in motion. On our side counter measures have been taken.

"The weight of the enemy's tanks has given him a penetration of a number of miles, deep into our front. When I left it two hours ago, the situation was still fluid."

"There is no doubt that the threat is a major one," Hottelot added. "It involves crack divisions and material."

THREAT TO ENTIRE FRONT

"It is intended to be a serious threat to our entire front. The enemy has more divisions right behind the front line with which to follow up his gains. He must have strained his operational reserves to the utmost.

"The Germans intend to break the back of our winter offensive with this stroke."

20 December 1944

FIRST HIT BACK IN BELGIUM

RAF BATTLE THROUGH FOG TO BOMB RUNDSTEDT'S SUPPLIES

BATTLING in dense fog alive with buzz-bombs and shells, U.S. First Army troops yesterday launched counter-attacks on German tank columns in Belgium and Luxembourg.

The fog grounded nearly all Allied and Luftwaffe fighter-bombers, but RAF and U.S. "heavies" from Britain plastered supply routes behind the attacking Germans.

The RAF went for Trier, southern end of the new front, and the Americans hit road and rail junctions near this town.

The SHAEF (and German) news black-out on army positions continued yesterday, fourth day of Rundstedt's counter-attack.

SHAEF's silence seemed to indicate that the First Army had not yet stabilised its line. According to an unconfirmed report broadcast by Paris, the Germans have recaptured the communications centre of Malmedy, thirteen miles inside Belgium.

DAVID WALKER cables from the U.S. Ninth Army front, in Germany, to which he returned yesterday from Belgium

It is important to realise that, although the German counter-attack against the First Army is employing a number of good divisions and probably a large number of tanks, strong German forces still stand opposite us here and opposite the British on our left flank.

It is revealing no secret – and shows the initial speed of the German advance – to say that a Panzer column, earlier reported to be several miles away, appeared on a hill overlooking my billet village THIRTY MINUTES AFTER MY DEPARTURE this morning.

⬥ General Eisenhower delivers a Christmas message to soldiers from each of the Allied countries in December 1944.

21 December 1944

POSITION IN BELGIUM "GRAVE"

HUNS SLAY UNARMED PRISONERS

THE Germans are slaughtering Americans they capture in their all-out drive into Belgium and Luxembourg.

First Army H.Q. are reporting to Washington confirmed accounts of these mass murders.

One such confirmed account of German tanks turning their guns and wiping out 125 American artillerymen and medical personnel who surrendered in the area of Monschau on Sunday was told by one of fifteen soldiers – all wounded – who escaped.

He said: "On December 17 our field artillery battery encountered German tanks on a road and were also fired at from the sides of the road.

"We sought cover but were ultimately taken prisoner.

"The men, some 140 of them, were robbed of their cigarettes and valuables and then ordered into a field with their hands up.

"Suddenly a single shot was fired at us, then tank machine-guns opened up, firing at all of us lying prostrate.

"Goebbels! Gobbles! Goebbels!—dat's der nearest ve'll get to a turkey this Xmas!"

"The shooting continued until a pile of dead and wounded were lying on the ground. I and other men feigned death and during a lull ran into a wood."

Another eye-witness account said that only a few miles from the scene of the first atrocity a second ruthless slaying of helpless prisoners took place under equally shocking conditions.

TANK MACHINE GUNS

A Nazi officer ordered the prisoners to be taken to an open field where, after being searched, they were told to hold their hands above their heads. Suddenly tank machine-guns poured lead up and down their lines until all were lying on the ground.

Then the bloody, screaming mass of American soldiers lying on the ground were further shot by individual Germans who were seeking to make sure that their death was final, cables Reuter correspondent John Wilhelm.

An American broadcast from Belgium yesterday described the situation in one area as "grave." Numbers of U.S. troops have been cut off near St. Vith, ten miles south of Malmedy, and seven miles inside Belgium, the broadcaster said.

"Our troops are caught in the German armoured pincers which have now carried the enemy to a point within three miles of St. Vith," he said.

MORALE OF GERMANS IS SOARING

From DAVID WALKER,
with the U.S. Ninth Army,
Wednesday

THE word "serious" was used this morning in reference to the German thrust into Belgium, while the situation is improving in parts.

The Germans still boast that places some distance behind our present line are their immediate objectives, and the fact must be faced that enemy morale appears to have soared in fighting areas.

Once and for all the British people must realise we are not fighting an army of beardless brats and gaga grenadiers.

At least one of their armoured thrusts has already gone through area which I was assured only three days ago on the spot was highly unfavourable to all armoured movement.

No estimates of enemy losses have yet been given us here, though they must certainly have been heavy in transport following our strikes from the air. But it is obvious that the Reichswehr is prepared to pay heavily in material.

We must recognise the situation as still serious, and it will require a maximum of effort on our part to prevent it from becoming more serious still: this is not pessimism but realism.

23 December 1944

"OUR GREATEST CHANCE" – IKE

"HUNS GAMBLE ALL, CAN BE DESTROYED"

WITH German divisions still driving west, General Eisenhower called yesterday for a supreme effort from all men of the Allied Expeditionary Forces.

The enemy counter-offensive, he said in an Order of the Day, is a bid to break out of the desperate plight into which he has been forced by the brilliant Allied victories of summer and autumn.

The enemy, he told the A.E.F., "is gambling everything, but already in this battle your gallantry has done much to foil his plans.

"In face of your proven bravery and fortitude he will completely fail.

"But we cannot be content with his mere repulse.

"By rushing out of his fixed defences, the enemy may give us the chance to turn his great gamble into his worst defeat.

"So I call upon every man of all the Allies to rise now to new heights of courage, resolution and effort.

"Let everyone hold before him the single thought – to destroy the enemy on the ground, in the air, everywhere – to destroy him.

"United in this determination and with unshakable faith in the cause for which we fight, we will, with God's help, go forward to our greatest victory."

Though some correspondents with the U.S. First Army yesterday said the German drive appeared to be blunted, Brussels radio reported violent tank battles on the outskirts of both Liege and Luxemburg city. A warning was flashed throughout Belgium yesterday by the military police that German soldiers, disguised in Belgian uniforms and civilian clothes, are moving about the country to commit sabotage. The Germans are using cars similar to those used by the Belgian official organisations, says Brussels radio.

"KEEP STOUT HEARTS AND CARRY ON" – MONTY

WE sing the Christmas hymns, full of hope, and steadfast in our belief that soon we shall achieve our heart's desire, says

Seasonal hangover

Field-Marshal Montgomery in his Christmas message to the 21st Army Group.

"Therefore, with faith in God, and with enthusiasm for our cause and for the day of battle, let us continue the contest with stout hearts and with determination to conquer."

"The forces of the British Empire in Western Europe spend Christmas, 1944, in the field," says Monty. "But what a change has come over the scene since last Christmas.

"Last Christmas we were in England, expectant and full of hope. This Christmas we are fighting in Germany.

"It would have needed a brave man to say on D-Day, June 6, that in three months we would be in Brussels and Antwerp, having liberated nearly the whole of France and Belgium, and in six months we would be fighting in Germany.

"But this is what has happened, and we must not fail to give the praise and honour where it is due: 'This was the Lord's doing, and it is marvellous in our eyes.'

"At Christmas time, whether in our homes or fighting in the field, we like to sing the carols we learnt as children; and in truth this is indeed a link between us and our families and friends in the home country, since they are singing the same verses.

"Wherever you may be, fighting in the front line or working on the lines of communication or in the ports, I wish all of you good luck and a happy 1945. We are all one great team, together, you and I. We have achieved much, and together we will see the thing through."

◆ German success in the Ardennes was short-lived and by the end of the year Hitler's defeat was only a matter of time.

29 December 1944

SQUEEZE TIGHTENS ON GERMAN 'NECK' IN BELGIUM

TRAPPED HUNS POUNDED

ALLIED guns were last night pouring concentrated fire into the large German force, spearhead of the drive to the Meuse, which has been chopped off and surrounded between Rochefort and Celles.

Allied armoured units were smashing into the Huns in the Celles area, taking many prisoners and inflicting heavy losses in men and equipment. Meanwhile the Allies have further squeezed the main German salient, have regained the initiative in an increasing number of sectors and are recapturing territory taken by the Germans in their advance.

The greatest Allied effort is being directed against the neck of the salient, where our troops are pressing in wedges from the north and south, threatening to chop off the big German force to the west.

On the southern flank the hinge town of Echternach has been taken by the Allies after hand-to-hand fighting.

Guenther Weber, military correspondent of the German Overseas News Agency, admitted last night that the Germans have gone over to "elastic defence" between Echternach and Bastogne.

On the northern flank the village of Manhay, seven miles north-east of La Roche and on the highway from Liege to Bastogne, is once more in American hands.

The Germans are attacking the relief corridor to Bastogne, but as

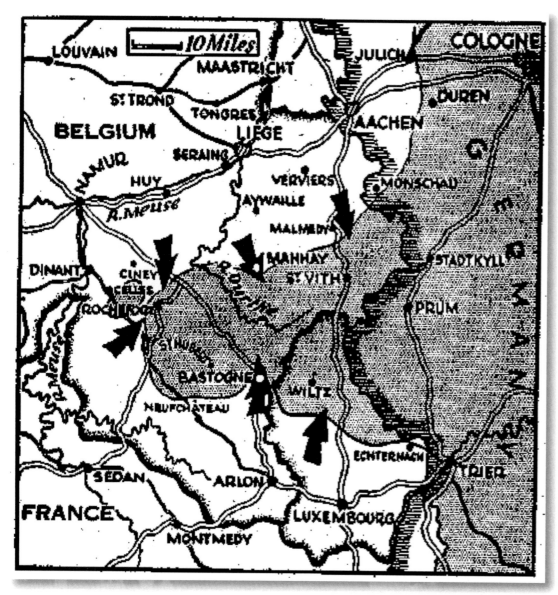

U.S. Eighth Air Force sent more than 1,200 Flying Forts and Liberators to bombard railway yards, bridges and other critical links in the transport network in rear of the salient.

BASTOGNE MEN GAVE THEIR ANSWER TO "SURRENDER" CALL IN ONE WORD. . ."NUTS!"

WITH the word "Nuts!" the besieged American garrison of Bastogne, Belgium, replied to a German ultimatum to surrender, it was revealed yesterday.

The surrender ultimatum gave the Americans two hours to decide. The Germans got their one-word answer in less than thirty minutes.

Three days later, on Christmas Day, the Germans bombarded the garrison with Christmas cards showing on one side an American soldier holding the hand of a little girl, who is saying "I'm frightened, daddy."

On the other side was a picture of Father Christmas saying: "Come over, boys. . . You'll get a merry Christmas here."

far as is known at SHAEF it is still held firmly.

There are signs that the Germans are trying to pull back the tip of their spearhead, one-third of the way across Belgium.

Apparently realising the danger to their rear, they have started large fires in the area north of St. Hubert, which may indicate that they are destroying equipment before pulling back.

In the Stavelot sector enemy engineers are kept busy laying mines to protect expected withdrawals.

Bitterly cold weather, with roads covered with snow and ice, make the going difficult.

Fog yesterday grounded nearly all our tactical air forces, but the

The battle for Bastogne began in a fog on the morning of December 19 when, according to the defenders, "all hell broke loose."

Rundstedt's forces attempted to overrun the town with attacks in mass formation. They paid dearly.

"We knocked them off like flies. Our artillery really did a butchering job on them," recalled a bearded sergeant from Chicago, who himself killed four attackers with the first hand grenade he threw.

Elements of one American division alone knocked out more than 105 German armoured vehicles in the first two days of the fighting.

Altogether, according to officers in Bastogne, the Wehrmacht lost nearly 200 tanks trying to crack the town's defences.

STALIN ACTS

Russia is making certain of civil peace in Hungary by sponsoring a government of several parties headed by General Bela Miklos. Representatives of this government are now in Moscow.

Stalin will invite Hungarians to join with Russia in the invasion of Germany through Austria and Czechoslovakia. He plans to encourage a similar provisional government in Austria.

30 December 1944

ALLIES DEEPER INTO 'BULGE'

WITH the Allies striking hard at the three sides of the German bulge in Belgium, Von Rundstedt was reported last night to be pulling out fast at some points.

On the northern front the Germans generally are breaking contact and withdrawing out of artillery range to regroup and refit after their mauling, says Reuter's correspondent with the U.S. forces.

It is suggested that the enemy may be preparing a new blow somewhere in the salient.

"It is imperative that we should realise that the Reichswehr has not yet shot its bolt and may have plenty more surprises for us," said David Walker in a battlefront message last night.

"It would be folly to believe that we can all now sit back again – on the contrary the moment has now come when the enemy must put into action whatever plan he has chosen during the present lull, and we know he has plenty of divisions with which to make another serious effort."

Later an ominous amount of German movement and the concentration of artillery was reported in several sectors.

While Rundstedt may be collecting his forces for another punch it is apparent, however, that his armour has taken a hammering.

159

The swing of the pendulum

It was estimated at SHAEF last night that he has lost 1,000 tanks in the past twelve days.

While the trapped German force west of Rochefort is being ground down by artillery, the Allies were reported last night to be advancing in the wake of retreating panzer columns east of Rochefort.

In the south, General Patton's forces have pushed to the German border six miles north-west of Echternach.

Patton has thrown at least eight divisions into his counter-attack, and his men yesterday maintained their three-miles-a-day advance.

In the north Allied forces are within five miles of one of the only two main roads left to Rundstedt to supply his forward units.

Both Allied armies coming from the north and from the south are already within artillery range of Houffalize, now the core of the enemy position.

Close support air forces were again grounded.

5 January 1945

LET THROUGH – INTO HELL

FIFTY German tanks and a regiment of infantry launched an attack due southwards against the northernmost tip of the Bastogne salient.

U.S. airborne troops deliberately let them through.

Then, as the Germans thought they were getting nicely into the Allied lines, hell broke loose.

Bazookas, direct artillery fire and tank destroyers smashed into the exposed flanks of the German lines.

Within a few hours the breakthrough had been crushed and sealed.

GIVE US FACTS, NOT FANTASY

From DAVID WALKER,
with United States Armies, Thursday

I'M writing this from the fighting line, but at the moment I am more concerned about the home front.

The attitude at home is of vital importance because the fighting line gets all its supplies from there.

Upon how the home front feels depends the supply of shells and tanks and aircraft.

IF THE HOME FRONT IS FOOLED INTO BELIEVING THAT THE WAR IS AS GOOD AS WON, HUMAN NATURE SEES TO IT THAT THIS DELIVERY DROPS.

AND IT IS MY PERSONAL CONVICTION, SHARED BY PEOPLE FAR MORE COMPETENT TO JUDGE, THAT YOU

AT HOME HAVE BEEN FOOLED.

In the first place, it is quite clearly not your fault. Your news comes to you from the radio and newspapers.

The radio and the newspapers get THEIR news from two sources: from high-powered experts in London, Paris and Brussels; and from representatives who spend their days more or less in the front line, working subject to an essential military censorship.

I think the trouble stretches right back to 1939, 1940 and 1941. It was when I was in Rumania in 1940 and 1941 that the world was informed from the files of the Ministry of Economic Warfare that Germany was in such a jam over petroleum that she couldn't really wage a full-scale war much longer. Take that as a starting point.

Jump all the well-known and unhappy interludes and come to 1944. When we were told of the desperate plight of German man-power; the destruction of all his communication systems; and the total eclipse of the Luftwaffe.

What makes it difficult is that each is based on a half-truth. The Hun is strained for man-power; his communications have been bombed like the devil; and the Luftwaffe had been silent for some time.

BUT THE OTHER HALF OF THE TRUTH IS THAT, NEVERTHELESS, SOME SIXTEEN FIRST-CLASS DIVISIONS WERE THROWN INTO THIS OFFENSIVE, WITH MORE IN RESERVE (DESPITE THE NEEDS OF THE RUSSIAN AND ITALIAN FRONTS); THAT HE CAN MOVE DIVISIONS AROUND WITH ASTONISHING SPEED; AND THAT THE LUFTWAFFE IS OUT IN FORCE AND ASKING FOR COMBAT.

My view (and I may be all wrong about this) is that we need a purge among the experts, both military and economic.

Since being out here I have attended conferences both British and American. Some were good and some were lousy.

And though I hate to have to say it, the British were the lousier of the two.

But both of them have a deplorable habit of giving you some items of good news for publication; and then saying something else, which the Germans probably know about, and sealing your wretched lips by telling you it's off the record.

I don't think this is so much unfair to us as damnably unfair to you.

SURELY THE WAR HAS REACHED A STAGE AT WHICH THE BRITISH AND AMERICAN PUBLIC CAN FACE THE FACTS. IF THEY HAD BEEN GIVEN THE REAL FACTS THE AMERICAN ARMY MIGHT NOT HAVE BEEN SHORT OF SHELLS AND THE BRITISH MIGHT HAVE IMMEDIATELY

REALISED THE REASON FOR CALLING UP ANOTHER 250,000 MEN.

Unfortunately I do not know all their names, but I have the feeling that there is quite a group of men, now firmly entrenched behind their exalted rank, who to my mind come into the category of opium laid cocaine smugglers.

What the Americans lightly call "dope" is, I believe, dope in our meaning of the word.

That is why I think there should be a purge. The digestion of these experts would all be greatly improved by a few weeks in the line.

Anybody who writes like this is open to the charge of sour grapes. We can let that ride.

FAR MORE IMPORTANT IS THAT YOU AT HOME DESERVE TO BE TREATED LIKE ADULTS AND TOLD THE TRUTH; PARTICULARLY FROM NOW ON. I wish I could give you more of it now.

The war would be over sooner if we stuck to facts and not fantasy; and fewer of our men would be killed.

TAKE BLINKERS OFF PUBLIC CALL BY PEER

"WE cannot be expected to fight this war in blinkers," declared Lord Strabolgi, speaking in London last night.

"The degree of political censorship now being exercised in the British military sphere in the Mediterranean and Middle East was becoming a positive danger," he said.

Information already known to the enemy and which in any case had no direct bearing on military operations was being kept from the public.

The Press had done a splendid job in this war and was not to be blamed.

6 January 1945

MONTY'S NEW JOB: HOW HUNS WERE HELD

GENERAL GEORGE MARSHALL, U.S. Chief of Staff, revealed in Washington last night that Field-Marshal Montgomery took over the command of the U.S. Ninth Army and most of the U.S. First Army on the second night of Rundstedt's counter-offensive in Belgium and Luxemburg.

That was on the exciting night of December 14–15, when no one, not even the Allied Supreme Command, knew exactly what was happening in the Ardennes.

It is still impossible to tell the full story of the most sensational change in command on the Western Front in this war.

But it is true to say that the change stopped the Germans from breaking through to the River Maas and beyond, possibly as far as Antwerp, the greatest Allied supply port.

British troops came south and swung into action in the nose of the salient as American troops held fast on the flanks.

SHAEF revealed last night that it was British troops which captured Bure, the tip of the salient, a few days ago.

They are now clearing the enemy from other towns and villages.

The decision to put the American troops attacking the northern flank under Monty's command had been known to correspondents at 21st Army Group H.Q. (Monty's H.Q.) since December 16.

But the censors treated it as one of the major secrets of the war.

It was feared that the Germans, knowing who was in command in each sector, might be able to anticipate what kind of counter-blow was coming.

THE GERMANS, HOWEVER, QUICKLY LEARNED OF THE CHANGE, AND ANNOUNCED THE DETAILS ALMOST AS SOON AS THEY WERE MADE.

ALLIED PINCERS ON THE ARDENNES SALIENT ARE ONLY TEN MILES APART

RUNDSTEDT'S PUSH IN SAAR BECOMES FULL OFFENSIVE

AMERICAN troops commanded by Field-Marshal Montgomery, attacking Rundstedt's Ardennes salient from the north, are now within ten miles of the U.S. Third Army, driving from the south, according to New York radio last night.

Monty's Americans are making headway against one German panzer and two German infantry divisions.

So far, the British have met stiff opposition, which is gradually increasing, but there has been no major effort on the part of the enemy to throw them back to their original positions.

The weather on the front yesterday was becoming clearer, but

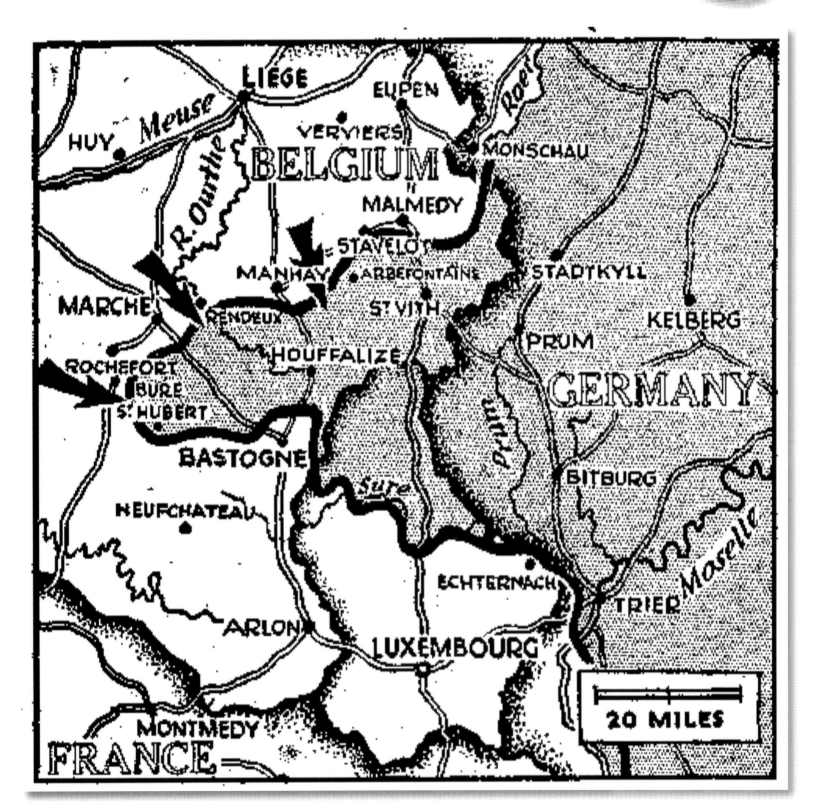

there were indications of a thaw coming.

British tanks and infantry, grinding their way through German minefields and stiff resistance, have advanced more than a mile and reached points three miles south of Hotten.

Earlier they were reported to have reached Surawha, a 3,000ft. tree-covered peak two miles south of the Hotten–Marche road, and Rendeux, eight miles north-east of Marche.

According to a Reuter message from SHAEF, Rundstedt's hacking at the Allied positions along the Saar Valley has now assumed the scale of a full-fledged offensive.

It is fully engaging the American Armies there and threatening a possible breakthrough into the Alsace and Lorraine plains.

CHURCHILL REVIEWS THE CAMPAIGN WITH "IKE"

It was announced last night: "The Prime Minister, accompanied by the Chief of the Imperial General Staff, returned this afternoon from a short visit to France, during which he met General Eisenhower and Field-Marshal Montgomery."

By BILL GREIG

MR. CHURCHILL'S visit to France was hastily arranged after consultation with President Roosevelt.

Various urgent questions of supply, both of man-power and munitions, arose immediately after the German breakthrough on the Western Front, and it was decided that the most satisfactory course was for the Prime Minister to have personal consultations with General Eisenhower and his chiefs of staff.

Strategic questions were discussed. Rundstedt's attack has changed the picture completely. In fact, had General Eisenhower been correct in his estimate of the German strength, we should by now have been at a period of guerrilla warfare.

One effect of Mr. Churchill's visit may be felt in our war factories.

8 January 1945

'WRITING HUNS OFF' – MONTY

FIELD-MARSHAL MONTGOMERY said yesterday that, though the battle of the Ardennes salient is by no means over yet, the enemy forces "are now being written off."

The Allies have now gained the initiative, he said.

Wearing the red beret and green jacket of the British Paratroops, Monty gave Press correspondents a confident survey of the position.

As he spoke, important gains were being made by the armies under his command, a tank force slashing across one of the enemy's two major east–west supply roads.

But last night Supreme H.Q. announced that the Germans have crossed the Maas and established a small bridgehead on the British side between Roermond and Venlo.

In the south the Germans have reinforced their bridgehead over the Rhine with both armour and infantry.

In the Saar, we have been forced to withdraw from Neunkirchen.

Monty, who paid generous tributes to General Eisenhower and the American forces, revealed that he took counter-measures to stop the enemy break-through before he was given command of all the Allied northern armies.

"When Rundstedt attacked on December 16 he obtained a tactical surprise" – the Field-Marshal said. "He drove a deep wedge into the centre of the First U.S. Army and the split might have become awkward: the Germans had broken right through a weak spot, and were heading for the Meuse.

"As soon as I saw what was happening I took certain steps myself to ensure that if the Germans got to the Meuse."

Monty has put Rundstedt's picture on the wall of his room, beside Rommel's.

"I used to think Rommel was good," he said yesterday, "but Von Rundstedt could 'knock him for six.'

"Rundstedt is the best general I've come up against in this war."

11 January 1945

BRITISH GO FORWARD 3 MILES

DRIVING forward up to three miles on a front of nearly ten miles, British forces have cut off the tip of Rundstedt's Ardennes salient.

They recaptured the village of Bure in some of the most savage fighting of the war, took four other villages and reached three more.

A spokesman at Field-Marshal Montgomery's headquarters later spoke of "a definite German pull-back" from the tip of the salient. But he emphasised, "It is not a gallop, but a measured withdrawal, step by step."

With American forces under Montgomery making headway on other parts of the northern flank of the salient, and the Third Army pushing in from the south, the Allied position in Belgium was very good yesterday.

But in Alsace the Germans now hold the initiative on a 100-mile front from the Saareguemines area to north of Colmar, though U.S.

counter-attacks have reduced their gains.

And the German radio claimed that the German Maas bridgehead near Wassum, north of Venlo, was still intact, though heavy British attacks are being made against it, it was admitted.

The British in Belgium are now going hammer and tongs over nightmarish country, pressing close behind the Germans, said a correspondent at Monty's H.Q. yesterday.

13 January 1945

BRITISH GO THROUGH, LINK UP

BRITISH troops under Field-Marshal Montgomery have joined up with Third Army forces from the south by meeting at St. Hubert, near the south-western corner of the German salient in Belgium.

The whole of the western tip of the salient has been cleared.

British forces report there are no Germans left west of the Laroche–St. Hubert road. This means that Rundstedt has pulled back twenty-three miles from the deepest point of penetration.

15 January 1945

BULGE "NOSE" IS BROKEN BY BRITISH

THREE Allied armies continue to fold up the German winter salient like an accordion, a Reuter correspondent reported late yesterday from the Ardennes battle area.

And with this announcement came more news of gains by British troops, who cut off the "nose" of the salient by capturing Champlon yesterday, and then linked up with American First Army columns as other U.S. forces cut the Houffalize–St. Vith road – last German escape line from the bulge.

The American armoured units drove 5,000 yards to cut the St. Vith road, and last night they were only 5,000 yards from Houffalize itself.

The battle has increased to a new ferocity, said the German High Command, reporting an American attack, several divisions strong, along the entire arc of the bulge.

Crack S.S. Panzer divisions, aided by Volksgrenadiers, are fighting like fury to give the rest of the rats time to run, cables David Walker, your correspondent.

Rundstedt is fighting a desperate withdrawal, but is still risking masses of armour and artillery, so that it won't be quick and it certainly won't be easy, he says.

Victory in Europe

The Battle of the Bulge proved merely a temporary hold-up in the Allied advance on Berlin. Once Montgomery, in charge of American troops, managed to halt Rundstedt's Nazi offensive, it was quickly turned back and German troops were in full retreat. The last barrier to the final defeat of Germany was the Rhine. The famous river was all that stood between Eisenhower's armies and the end of the war.

◀ An American soldier looks on as a Russian counterpart finds a bronze bust of Adolf Hitler in the remains of the Reichstag in Berlin.

DAILY MIRROR, Friday, January 19, 1945.

No. 12,819
ONE PENNY
Registered at the G.P.O. as a Newspaper.
JAN 19

RED ARMY ARE INTO GERMANY

Churchill's hint to Hun

By Your Political Correspondent

INTENSE interest was shown last night in that section of the Prime Minister's speech in which, for the first time, he gave a hint that the terms following unconditional surrender might not be so severe as the Germans have been led to expect.

It was the first invitation from an Allied leader to the Germans asking them to surrender and at the same time holding out hope for the future.

There can be no doubt that it was done after consultation with President Roosevelt, and much significance was attached to the words used.

The Prime Minister, declaring that there could be no negotiation with Germany or Japan until they surrendered unconditionally, went on : " We may say to our foes we demand unconditional surrender, but you will know how strict are the moral limits within which we are bound.

" We make no bargain with you. We accord you nothing as a right. Abandon your resistance unconditionally, we remain bound by our customs and nature. Several countries have already surrendered unconditionally. Already there is a tolerable life for their people.

" In Italy, for instance, sometimes one has almost wondered whether it was we who had surrendered unconditionally to them."

Mr. Churchill said the enemy could also be told that if they surrendered now, their suffering after the war would not be comparable with what they would otherwise have to endure in 1945.

Although, in his speech, Mr. Churchill emphasised that victory might be distant and would certainly be costly, it is believed he feels the possibility of an appeal to the German people having some success is greater than at any time in the past.

On the war situation he declared : " The whole Eastern and Western fronts, and the long front in Italy, will be kept henceforward in constant flame until the final climax is reached."

His verdict on the Western Front was this: " In my opinion the decisive breaking of the German offensive is more likely to lengthen the war than to lengthen it."

He believed also that the enemy, in attempting to dislocate the forthcoming Anglo-American offensive, had not only lost large forces which he could not replace, but had failed to delay " the doom closing in on them from the West."

PREMIER'S SPEECH AND DEBATE: BACK PAGE

LUBLIN POLES TAKE OVER IN A WARSAW DECKED WITH FLAGS

FLAGS fluttered from every building when the Polish Provisional Government entered and took over the administration of Warsaw yesterday, Their leader, M. Osbuka-Moravsky, took possession of the Parliament House, according to Lublin radio.

Citizens held a solemn meeting to mark the liberation of the capital, while at Lublin, where the Government was first formed, artillery salvos were fired to celebrate the victory, added the broadcast.

Meantime, behind the German lines, says Moscow radio, panic has broken out among civilians and high Nazi party officials are evacuating their private belongings.

150 DEAD IN SMASH

One hundred and fifty dead have been taken from the ruins of the station of St. Valery-en-Caux, near Dieppe, where a train over-ran the buffers. The train smashed the station

Old men and boys of Home Guard were Nazi 'barrier' to the Russian invasion

FIRST waves of the great Russian onslaught have swept over the Reich border in Upper Silesia and the Red Army was last night fighting on German soil.

Koniev's tanks and lorry-borne infantry, racing on from Czestochowa, are the new Russian spear thrust into the side of Germany. They are less than 50 miles from Breslau, great Silesian industrial centre, which is now directly threatened.

And last night Willi Michels, German official News Agency war correspondent, said that the shock of the Russian invasion was met by members of the Volkssturm, the German Home Guard.

" These are hard times for the soldiers of the Volkssturm," he said. " They are going through most bitter fighting, these men of fifty, and more years of age, and youngsters of sixteen and seventeen, the miner, peasants, the shopkeepers and Civil Servants."

Marshal Stalin told last night of a fresh victory for Marshal Rokossovsky's armies.

Sweeping north round Warsaw, on a 40-mile front, they have broken through to the Lower Vistula, and last night were poised for a crossing to link up with Zhukov in the massive thrust to the west.

Modlin, fortress town on the east bank of the Lower Vistula, twenty miles north-west of Warsaw, has fallen.

Rokossovsky's columns at the other end of his front have struck west to reach Krasnysz, seventeen miles south of the East Prussian border, and seized over 1,000 other towns and villages.

Zhukov's forces have taken Lowicz, forty miles west of Warsaw.

The Red armies, their offensives accelerating at top speed, are charging west across the Polish plain, overrunning hysterical German groups

The battle is completely fluid and on all the main sectors the Germans are being thrown back wily-nilly.

Berlin commentators are increasingly gloomy.

Von Olberg, admitting that German forces have been swamped by the Soviet advance, stated : " To call a halt to the attackers, time is needed.

Soviet bomber formations were over Silesia last night.

Monty's tanks through

BERLIN REPORTS

British tanks have broken through the German defences in the Roer River bridgehead (Cologne front), and German motorised commandos are in action against them.—Official German News Agency.

BATTLING on the doorstep of the Reich, under a dreary drizzle and through mine - infested mud. British Second Army infantry yesterday advanced more than half a mile east of Echt in the direction of the Roermond - Sittard road, according to a message from Field - Marshal Montgomery's H.Q.

Some troops have reached that highway, widened their original line of attack, and cleared Oudroosteren, northwest of Dieteren.

Pushing forward more than a mile towards the village of Hongen in a new movement north-east of Sittard, they have " seen off " a small German counter-attack on the Roermond-Sittard road.

They met heavy opposition everywhere, but German tanks nowhere.

In admitting the British " breakthrough," the German News Agency said that three British divisions, including one tank division, were attacking the Roer bridgehead.

To the south, it was stated, British troops in the Gellenkirchen sector (where they link with the U.S. Ninth Army) were being reinforced.

According to Berlin, also, British troops, supported by

M.T.Bs. and assault boats, landed on the Dutch island of Schouwen yesterday morning.

" The British forces were halted by German covering troops and then were wiped out, apart from small remnants which withdrew," it was stated.

Schouwen Island lies north of North Beveland and is separated from it by the East Scheldt, at this point between six and seven miles wide.

At the north end of the Ardennes salient, American troops, slowly advancing through chest-deep snow along the Ligneu-

ville-St. Vith road, are now three and a half miles from St. Vith.

At the southern end of the salient, two divisions of the U.S. Third Army yesterday launched a new attack, crossing the Sure River from the south near Dickirch, fifteen miles north of Luxemburg.

This attack is presenting a new threat to the bastion town of Wiltz, for which the " Third " has been aiming since it became apparent that the Germans might use it as the southern anchor of a defence line.

UTILITY FURNITURE
DEARER AGAIN

Retail prices of utility beds and tables have been increased " to cover a rise in costs of materials and labour."

A £4 7s. 3d. bedstead will cost £4 4s. 6d. after January 25. A £3 3s. 6d. kitchen table goes up to £4, and a £5 15s. 3d. dining table to £6 3s.

Last increases in utility furniture prices were in September, 1944, " to give the makers a fairer margin of profit."

TWO ACCUSED OF COFFIN THEFT

TWO men appeared at Darlington (Durham) yesterday on charges of coffin stealing. The case was adjourned till February 14 and the men allowed bail.

They were fifty-nine-year-old Paul Bowman, of Bates-avenue, Darlington, furnaceman at the local crematorium, and William Hirstwood, forty-nine-year-old joiner and undertaker, of Eastbourne-road, Darlington.

The men were jointly charged with the larceny of ten coffin lids from Darlington Crematorium and with conspiracy over a period to steal other coffin lids. Hirstwood was separately charged with larceny of other lids.

The dates upon which the alleged offences were committed were November 1 and December 1, 1943.

Both men pleaded not guilty, and for the defence it was said that the men had full explanations which they would give at the proper time

17 January 1945

40 MILES OFF REICH, SOVIET SWEEP ON

RED ARMY'S GREAT LEAP FORWARD

RUSSIAN forces are only forty miles from Germany. Marshal Koniev's troops have crashed forward thirty miles in a day from Kielce in Southern Poland and are mounting an immediate threat to the Reich border.

Forcing the River Pilica on a front over thirty miles wide and capturing Koniecpol, Marshal Koniev's troops are sweeping on to the west only twenty-five miles from Czestochowa, an important junction on the approaches to Silesia.

South-west of Kielce, armoured columns stabbing out for Cracow, second city of Poland, are only twelve miles away at one point.

The communiqué announcing these gains followed two Orders of the Day from Marshal Stalin announcing a new big breakthrough by Marshal Zhukov's First White Russian Army on a seventy-five-mile wide front south of Warsaw.

18 January 1945

WARSAW

WARSAW, Europe's most tragic city, came out of the shadows yesterday.

It fell to the Red Army after more than five years of German occupation – five years of torture which were made even more dreadful by the death and devastation of four savage battles.

Before the war the city had a population of 1,200,000. Its people have been decimated by war, hunger, and disease, and by murder and deportation.

19 January 1945

CHURCHILL'S HINT TO HUN

By YOUR POLITICAL CORRESPONDENT

INTENSE interest was shown last night in that section of the Prime Minister's speech in which, for the first time, he gave a hint that the terms following unconditional surrender might not be so severe as the Germans have been led to expect.

It was the first invitation from an Allied leader to the Germans asking them to surrender and at the same time holding out hope for the future.

There can be no doubt that it was done after consultation with President Roosevelt, and much significance was attached to the words used.

The Prime Minister, declaring that there could be no negotiation with Germany or Japan until they surrendered unconditionally, went on: "We may say to our foes we demand unconditional surrender, but you will know how strict are the moral limits within which we are bound.

"We make no bargain with you. We accord you nothing as a right. Abandon your resistance unconditionally, we remain bound by our customs and nature.

"Several countries have already surrendered unconditionally. Already there is a tolerable life for their people.

"In Italy, for instance, sometimes one has almost wondered whether it was we who had surrendered unconditionally to them."

Mr. Churchill said the enemy could also be told that if they surrendered now, their suffering after the war would not be comparable with what they would otherwise have to endure in 1945.

27 January 1945

ALLIES TAKE A GERMAN TOWN WITHOUT A FIGHT

For the first time since the Allies began to battle in GERMANY, the Huns gave up territory yesterday without a fight.

They hardly fired a shot to defend the Roer River town of Brachelen, which was captured by British tanks and infantry of the U.S. Ninth Army in a mile and a half advance. The Huns had retreated across the Roer.

At the same time, General Dempsey's men, after eleven days of slogging through ice and snow, had closed well up to the Wurm and Roer Rivers.

Those successes mean that the enemy has lost his last hold on the west bank of the Roer, one of the river barriers to any direct thrust towards Cologne or the Ruhr.

From GEORGE McCARTHY,
Western Front, Friday

THE battle for the line of the Roer River is virtually ended. With the capture of Heinsberg, the last important communications centre is in our hands.

Today we occupy a new string of villages, including Dremmen and the hamlet of Hoven, where weeks ago British infantry fought a

bitter battle and emerged with few survivors from a band of heroes.

This river battle has been no blitzkreig. Indeed it has gone more slowly than was at one time expected, but that is hardly surprising in view of the deep snow and frozen roads.

It has been marked – and this is no line shooting – by the remarkably small number of casualties we have suffered and by the high performance of our artillery.

The gunners have brought to something like perfection a system of timing with the swooping aircraft of the R.A.F.

This has frequently been used with devastating effect.

◀ Allied planes fly over the ruins of a German town on their way to drop paratroopers over the Rhine.

30 January 1945

"AS WE WERE" ON WEST FRONT

From DAVID WALKER,
Supreme Headquarters,
Monday

THIS IS where I came in. It is curious to be back here at headquarters and find that our line is almost exactly what it was when I passed through last November.

The main Siegfried Line, marked in heavy black on H.Q. maps, still lies just east of our various armies.

It is easy to understand why the Russians are again asking for an offensive in the West.

We are advancing slowly – the U.S. First Army have pushed forward through heavy snow to gain between one and two miles, and reach the outskirts of Bullingen (ten miles east of Malmedy), a little village I was in about the middle of December – but it is all small stuff compared to Red Army news.

The truth is that we are today edging our way back to the German frontier, meeting nothing but rearguard actions and the inevitable minefields.

We should also soon be back on the west bank of the Roer River on much the same scale as we were before.

With the French First Army south of the Colmar pocket, flame-throwers have been in action in Alsace villages today, and there, too, it's a question of getting back to "as you were."

Considering our enormous resources on paper, it is queer to think that the front line in the West is still where it was three months ago.

31 January 1945

HE MUST RUSH BACK

Marshal Stalin will have to hurry back from the forthcoming "Big Three" talks, said Mr. Harry Hopkins, President Roosevelt's personal adviser, in Rome yesterday.

For Stalin, he pointed out, is the actual director of the whole Russian strategy, and could not be long away from the vital front.

He added that it was not known in either Britain or America just how powerful the Russian offensive is, or whether the Germans can halt it.

Asked if Russia would declare war on Japan, Mr. Hopkins said that British and American plans to beat Japan were based on the assumption that only British and American military resources would be available.

"Nothing to declare!"

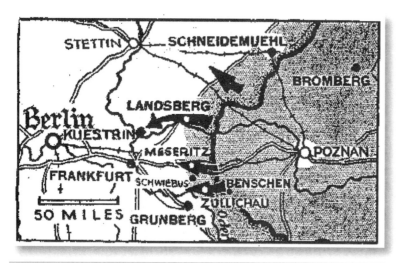

"TERRIBLE BATTLE IS NEAR"

50 MILES INSIDE REICH

AS the Red Army reached the Oder, just over forty miles from Berlin, Soviet planes swept over the river yesterday to bomb and strafe great columns of reinforcements the Germans were bringing up from the direction of their capital.

The official German communiqué, admitting the Russians had advanced to the Oder north-west of Kuestrin – over fifty miles west of the Reich border – said fresh reserves had been thrown in to check them there.

"A terrible battle is in the making at the Oder, with the Germans preparing for an all-out stand to save Berlin," said a Moscow message.

BIG 3 MEET: THE FINAL BLOW IS PLANNED

CHURCHILL, Stalin and Roosevelt are in conference "in the Black Sea area." They have already reached complete agreement on joint military operations to end the war against Germany.

This was revealed in an announcement made simultaneously in London, Moscow and Washington last night.

This statement was issued:

Mr. Roosevelt, Marshal Stalin and Mr. Churchill, accompanied by their Chiefs of Staff, the three Foreign Secretaries and other advisers, are now meeting in the Black Sea area.

"Their purpose is to concert plans for completing the defeat of the common enemy and for building, with their Allies, firm foundations for lasting peace.

Meetings are proceeding continuously."

FUTURE OF GERMANY

"The conference began with military discussions. The present situation on all the European fronts has been reviewed and the fullest information interchanged.

"THERE IS COMPLETE AGREEMENT FOR JOINT MILITARY OPERATIONS IN THE FINAL PHASE OF THE WAR AGAINST NAZI GERMANY.

"THE MILITARY STAFFS OF THE THREE GOVERNMENTS ARE NOW ENGAGED IN WORKING OUT JOINTLY THE DETAILED PLANS.

"Discussions of problems involved in establishing a secure peace have also begun.

"These discussions will cover joint plans for the occupation and control of Germany, the political and economical problems of liberated Europe and proposals for the earliest possible establishment of a permanent international organisation to maintain peace.

"A communiqué will be issued at the conclusion of the conference."

▶ Winston Churchill, Roosevelt and Stalin at the Yalta conference in February 1945.

LESS 'SPUDS' FOR ARMY

ARMY ration scales have been changed, the potato ration going down from 20 ozs. to 12 ozs. a head daily, and flour up from one and three-quarter ozs. to three and a quarter ozs.

The ATS potato ration goes down from 12 ozs. to eight, and flour up from two ozs. to two and three-quarters.

Extra split peas will go to all who get less potatoes.

GERMANS STILL HOPING

From DAVID WALKER,
outside Schmidt, Germany,
Thursday

ALTHOUGH London has not yet been completely destroyed, its inhabitants have gone crazy with fear and panic – according to

prisoners taken in Schmidt.

I have spent a couple of hours today with German infantry, just captured by United States 78th Division in this battle for Schmidt, in an attempt to solve one of the vexed problems of this crucial moment of the war: What exactly are the German troops thinking and saying about the news?

I have been talking with both private and officer class, and some of their answers flatly contradict previous reports.

The men were aged from 17 to 35, and did not include any S.S. troops. Here is what they say:

1. Russian troops are fighting in Kustrin and Frankfurt, and have crossed the Oder in force. (This was known to every single man questioned.)
2. We have not had any special gas training in recent weeks. We have always been ordered, particularly in Russia, to keep our gasmasks at our side.
3. If the Anglo-Americans start an offensive in the West today, you can rest assured that they will find German troops thick in all the country behind us.
4. Whoever wins the war, it is certain that Britain has lost it. The Russians will never leave what territory they occupy, even Berlin.
5. Of course the Fuehrer is alive. But he may have been temporarily ill after the bomb outrage.

All these men had fought well, some after being surrounded for some time. They prove that, even with full knowledge of the course of the war in the east, there are and will be plenty of tough fighters to contend with.

Of the last 5,000 prisoners falling to the 78th Division, one solitary soldier has said, "Heil Hitler," and he was described as a "middle-aged philosopher suffering from the delusion that Hitler was God." Not one of them could see HOW Germany could win the war, yet at least half of them expressed faith that she would win somehow.

Every single one wanted to be sent to the United States, but none of them to England.

◀ British troops entertain German children in February 1945.

13 February 1945

BIG THREE DECIDE ON NEW BLOWS AT HEART OF GERMANY FROM EAST, WEST, NORTH, SOUTH BY LAND AND AIR

"NEVER AGAIN" FETTERS FOR HUN

UNITY among Britain, Russia and America for the defeat, occupation and treatment of Germany, and on organisation for world peace, was agreed upon by Mr. Churchill, Marshal Stalin and President Roosevelt at their conference.

They met for eight days in a beautiful palace at Yalta, in the Crimea, and each of them was accompanied by key political Ministers and key commanders of each Power's land, sea and air forces.

The timing, scope and co-ordination of new blows from EAST, WEST, NORTH AND SOUTH have been planned in detail by the military staffs – who will meet whenever necessary in the future, and whose conversations have already shortened the war.

Unconditional surrender terms to be imposed on Germany will not be revealed until her defeat is complete.

Each of the three great Powers will occupy a separate zone – and France will be asked to take over a fourth.

There will be a joint H.Q. for the Allied Supreme Commanders in Berlin.

Britain, Russia and America are determined to crush Nazism, German militarism – including the Hun General Staff – control all war industry, bring all criminals to justice, and exact reparation in kind.

But they have no intention of destroying the German people.

▶ An RAF bomber attacks a Bremen oil refinery in March 1945.

STEADY DOES IT

THE war goes well. Big Russian forces are over the Oder. The threat to Berlin increases. On the Western side Anglo-American armies are making progress, slow but of immense strategic importance. We have every right to feel cheerful. That, however, is no reason why we should also be stupid. The war is going to end before long, but not so soon as many seem to think. Our duty is not to throw our hats up, but still to take our coats off and keep on with the job.

We make these cautionary remarks in no grudging spirit, but because that national pest the crass-optimist is about again. Give him an inch and he takes a mile. His most recent emotional manifestation was to mark off the distance of the Russians from Berlin. Day by day he deducted his mileage – fifty, forty-five, forty! Then the character of the attack changed and he came to a stop. But this made no difference to his enthusiasm. It was a case of "any minute now," and doubtless he prepared to indulge in celebrations.

WHEN BERLIN FALLS

Let us be more sensible than this foolish gentleman, and view events with common sense. There have been these "bull" periods before. Victory has been in sight several times before. Sometimes it has been the end of the beginning; sometimes it has been the beginning of the end. You pays yer money and you takes yer choice. Yet the war has gone on. Neither will the capture of Berlin itself mean that it is over. This war is like no other war. Its end will be like no other end. There may be no formal armistice or "peace" because there is no one to make it with. Possibly the Allies will have, slowly and completely, to occupy the country. No one can definitely say. We should be well advised, therefore, to dilute our heady hopes with a dash of sober realism. We may hope that we are not far off, but we know we are not there yet. Even when we are, there will be the most unholy mess in Europe to clear up. The killing by bombs and bullets will have ended, but not the killing by starvation, disease and fanaticism.

14 February **1945**

"BERLIN MAYOR EXECUTED"

Moscow radio, quoting Stockholm reports, said last night that the Mayor of Berlin, Ludvig Steeg, had been shot for cowardice. He is reported to have tried to leave Berlin, but was recognised, arrested and executed.

▶ German civilians leave the Rhineland town of Erkelenz in March 1945 after its capture by the Allies.

1 March **1945**

GOEBBELS HINTS AT SUICIDE OF HITLER "IF WE LOSE WAR"

GOEBBELS told the German people in a broadcast last night what would happen if Germany is defeated.

"The sufferings of all of us," he said, "would be such that obviously our leadership would choose death for themselves."

"Germany must reconquer the territory which she has lost in the East," he declared. "We will die rather than capitulate."

Among the threats he voiced to the Allies he forecast a strong resumption of U-boat activity and V-bombing of "ever wider areas of the British Isles."

◗ British soldiers of the Second Army enjoy a moment's peace in Reichswald Forest.

2 March 1945

HUNS STAND NEAR RHINE

From GEORGE McCARTHY,
inside Germany, Thursday

BITTER German resistance continued all day today on the British and Canadian front between the rivers.

To the southward the enemy's whole front is vanishing as the American armoured columns take giant strides northward.

By every teaching of war the moment has arrived when the Germans should rescue what troops they can and race for the crossings of the Rhine.

Instead, they stand and fight with the courage of despair.

In the Hoch Forest and in the gap where the Canadians two days ago pierced the last Siegfried defence, enemy Tiger tanks and self-propelled guns have fought a savage delaying action with such success that the Canadians tonight cannot report any advance.

There has been hard fighting, too, in the forest itself where Canadian infantry, striking south to link up with the troops in the gap, have been counter-attacked and held by heavy artillery fire and the soft mud in the woods.

Only in one vital place tonight is the enemy group being weakened.

At Kervenheim, key to the centre of the line, British infantry have fought their way into the streets and are now engaged in clearing the town.

Its capture is not yet claimed.

And further eastward British armour, with its accompanying infantry, has cut a swathe through tight German defences and now sits on the high ground dominating Sonsbeck. But nowhere is the enemy yielding ground without strong resistance.

IT'S REAL TIMING

Real synchronisation of the offensives in the East and West has taken place "for the first time," Moscow radio said yesterday.

And President Roosevelt told the U.S. Congress that one result of the Yalta Conference was the provision for a daily exchange

The devastation caused by RAF bombing to a large factory and rail-yard in the centre of Hanover.

FLAG OF RUIN FLIES AGAIN

The approaches to Munchen-Gladbach, some six miles long by three broad, are scarred with the ruins of huge factories. Stocks from shops are scattered in the roadways. Here and there is a tram, bullet-riddled.

When I drove into the town after its capture, writes a correspondent with the U.S. troops, I found the civilians looking dazed and dull, holding white flags, white handkerchiefs, anything white.

The homeless were dragging little carts containing what few possessions they had saved. There was ruin everywhere.

Civilians stood hopelessly at street corners.

In another Rhineland town, now in our hands, the bodies of a family of three were found hanging from the rafters of the sitting-room. A note said, "The shame of the German defeat was too much to bear."

3 March **1945**

"MONTY REGROUPS FOR LOWER RHINE ATTACK"

Field-Marshal Montgomery is carrying out a large-scale regrouping of his forces south-east of Emmerich for a crossing of the Lower Rhine, the German Official News Agency said last night.

"Most of the new units are formations of the British Second Army," the agency stated.

"NO PLEASURE MOTOR CARS FOR 2 YEARS"

THERE will be no new motor-cars for pleasure use for the next two years, Mr. A.F. Palmer Phillips, director of sales, Vauxhall Motors, forecast in Edinburgh last night.

"Many people believe that cars are just around the corner," he said. "That is not so. Cars are going to be controlled for some time to come."

There would be a small number of British cars available next year, but he did not think there would be any this year.

of information between the armies under command of General Eisenhower, those under the command of the Soviet marshals on the Eastern Front and our armies in Italy.

This exchange is carried out without the necessity of going through the Chiefs of Staff in Washington and London as in the past. From now on, the President declared, American and British heavy bombers will be used in the day-by-day tactics in direct support of the Soviet armies as well as in support of our own western front.

The German industrial town of Krefeld shows the effects of heavy RAF bombing.

BERLIN AGAIN – 10TH NIGHT RUNNING

BERLIN and Erfurt were attacked last night by Mosquitoes of RAF Bomber Command.

And as Berlin's "Achtung" was given – for the tenth successive night – a "ghost" voice in the background shouted: "End this air raid agony. Down with the war!"

Earlier, the German radio had reported a seventy-mile-long stream of fast bombers entering the province of Brandenburg, in which Berlin is situated. RAF and Australian Spitfire bomber formations battled through extremely bad weather over the Netherlands yesterday to continue the attack on rocket-objectives.

Any production this year would be wanted for export and for Government use.

There might be a priority for doctors.

Prices were going to be high.

PRINCESS ELIZABETH JOINS ATS WITH A COMMISSION

PRINCESS ELIZABETH has joined the ATS. She is training as an officer-driver.

The following official announcement was made at Buckingham Palace last night:

"The King has granted to Her Royal Highness the Princess Elizabeth a commission with the honorary rank of second subaltern in the Auxiliary Territorial Service.

"Her Royal Highness is at present attending a course at a driving-training centre in the South of England."

This step has been taken at the Princess's own request.

Last year, before her 18th birthday, it was decided that she should not for the time join any of the women's services, because her training as heiress presumptive was regarded as more important.

By the King's orders Princess Elizabeth is to receive no special privileges.

◀ Princess Elizabeth, as Junior Commander in the ATS, inspects the Motor Transport Training Centre at Camberley, Surrey.

PREMIER LUNCHES IN GERMAN TOWN

From DAVID WALKER,
Julich, Saturday (delayed)

WITHOUT awaiting a formal invitation from the Fuehrer, Mr. Churchill lunched here in Germany today.

He had to eat it in the open air at the entrance to a four-centuries old citadel because here in Julich we have only got open air to offer.

The Germans in Aachen seemed totally unaware of their visitor, and, headed by British military police, the little convoy passed through one destroyed German village after another to the Bailey bridge over the Roer and the fantastic ruins of Julich itself.

Montgomery pointed out the desolation. The Premier promptly

replied: "There won't be any unemployment here after the war."

NEXT day, according to Reuter, Mr. Churchill inspected officers and men of the 51st Highland Division in Germany, and declared:

"Soon we shall be across the Rhine. Anyone can see that one good strong heave all together will end the war in Europe."

▶ Winston Churchill and Field-Marshal Montgomery (left) outside the citadel at Julich.

10 March **1945**

10 MINS. WON BRIDGE: LONE COMPANY WENT RIGHT INTO HUN ARMY

THE story of the capture of the bridge at Remagen, ten minutes before the charges were due to go off which would blow it up, was told last night.

It is a story of deathless glory for one lone infantry company marched across the bridge, expecting at any moment to be blown to pieces. One company opened a hole in the German Army.

A U.S. tank reached the bridge just ten minutes, according to German civilians, from the hour fixed for its destruction.

Two young second-lieutenants, John Mitchell and John Mott, found and quickly disconnected the wires attached to the explosive charges. They called men to repair superficial damage while the bridge was under fire.

"BRIDGE SEIZED: FORCES CROSSING"

"A" Company of the 27th Infantry Battalion, part of the Ninth Armoured Division – the Phantoms – was first across.

Second Lieutenant J. Burrows, leader of the second platoon of "A" Company, went over while the battalion commander, Major Murray Deevers, stood at the edge and prayed.

"I was afraid the bridge would be blown up in our faces," said Major Deevers.

But Second Lieutenant Burrows got across. Lieutenant Timmerman, commanding "A" Company, followed.

Infantrymen swarmed to the capture of the town of Erpel.

"Bridge seized: Forces crossing" was the message that electrified Army Headquarters.

The Germans were stunned. Two prisoners were taken on the bridge itself, and within a few hours, hundreds were laying down their weapons.

DAILY MIRROR, Saturday, March 10, 1945.

Daily Mirror

MAR 10

No. 12,862
ONE PENNY
Registered
at the G.P.O.
as
a Newspaper.

Two armies shut trap on Nazis:
250 big guns batter the Ruhr

BATTLE OPENS ACROSS RHINE.

This is it!

↑ This picture shows one of the historic places in this war—the railway bridge at Remagen, seized intact by a handful of men whose daring broke the Rhine barrier to the Reich. Now American troops are pouring over the bridge in force. The cameraman reached the spot as soldiers were filling in the rail lines to make a "road."

GERMAN counter-attacks by land and air have begun on our Remagen bridgehead across the Rhine.

Reporting this last night, correspondents at Supreme Allied Headquarters said they had been unsuccessful.

Meanwhile another great success for the Allies was announced.

The U.S. First and Third Armies, linking up at two points on the west bank of the river eight and thirteen miles south of Remagen, have closed the trap on German forces estimated at between five and six divisions.

The Allied bridgehead is now certainly five miles wide, on German reports which speak of fighting at Linz and Unkel.

A report from Paris said it was ten miles wide and five miles deep. A German claim to have recaptured Unkel is not borne out.

The U.S. Third and First Armies met at Brohl and Andernach, which is a Rhine ferry terminus.

Mayen, sixteen miles west of Coblenz, was also captured. But all the bridges on the Third Army front had been blown up.

'A German divisional

Continued on Back Page

10 mins. won bridge: Lone company went right into Hun Army

THE story of the capture of the bridge at Remagen, ten minutes before the charges were due to go off which would blow it up, was told last night.

It is a story of deathless glory for one lone infantry company, which marched across the bridge, expecting at any moment to be blown to pieces. One company opened a hole in the German Army.

A U.S. tank reached the bridge just ten minutes, according to German civilians, from the hour fixed for its destruction.

Two young second-lieutenants, John Mitchell and John Mott, found and quickly disconnected the wires attached to the explosive charges. They called men to repair superficial damage while the bridge was under fire.

"Bridge Seized: Forces Crossing"

"A" Company of the 27th Infantry Battalion, part of the Ninth Armoured Division—the Phantoms—was first across.

Second Lieutenant J. Burrows, leader of the second platoon of "A" Company, went over while the battalion commander, Major Murray Deevers, stood at the edge and prayed.

"I was afraid the bridge would be blown up in our faces," said Major Deevers.

But Second Lieutenant Burrows got across. Lieutenant Timmerman, commanding "A" Company, followed. Infantrymen swarmed to the capture of the town of Erpel.

"Bridge seized: Forces crossing" was the message that electrified Army Headquarters.

The Germans were stunned. Two prisoners were taken on the bridge itself, and within a few hours, hundreds were laying down their weapons.

The debt

MR. ERNEST BEVIN, Minister of Labour, speaking in London yesterday, said he now had the poignant duty of filling the gaps in the Armies caused by the casualty lists.

"No one can look through those lists week after week without their hearts going out in gratitude to that great body of men—our famous infantry," he said.

"The greatest price is paid by those men.

"Sometimes they are regarded as the labourers of the Services, but I hope they will not be placed in that category when they come back."

See—The Day Goes Well: Page 2.)

NEW WARSHIP TASTES BLOOD

Britain's latest aircraft carrier, Implacable, sister ship of the Indefatigable, has been in battle, it is revealed today, one of her first operations being against the Admiral von Tirpitz.

With other Home Fleet ships she also carried out a number of strikes against enemy shipping off the Norway coast, during which upwards of sixteen enemy ships were either sunk or seriously damaged.

DAVID WALKER SAYS IT'S CRAZY THERE

BONN, Friday.

THIS thing is becoming crazier and crazier. With their dead still lying in the streets, with the shells still whining overhead and with the riverside suburbs still being mopped up, people of this famous University city seem pleased to see us.

The fighting here has been the stiffest that this U.S. First Division has had since Aachen, much of it house-to-house, while there was really tough fighting for the barracks, yet the people are out in the streets willing to guide and help us.

I went straight to the town hall, where I was rather alarmed to find three German uniformed policemen at the door; however, they saluted smartly and I went in to try to find the mayor.

The staff was all present and one of the girl secretaries with a sense of humour gave me a "welcome to Bonn" booklet written in English.

She said she was sorry I could not see the mayor because the old-so-and-so had escaped across the Rhine last night. But would I care to see the chief of police?

Later I went out to see the university, guarded by one group of Germans after another, and they explained without bitterness how it had been destroyed by the RAF, though Beethoven's house still miraculously stands. It was hard to believe that all this morning we had been fighting

STOKING IT UP

Berlin was attacked last night by the largest force of RAF bombers since the present series of night attacks began. It was the 228th raid on the Reich capital.

Continued on Back Page

➡ Allied armies hand out rations left behind by retreating German forces in a newly captured Rhine town.

DAVID WALKER SAYS IT'S CRAZY THERE

THIS thing is becoming crazier and crazier. With their dead still lying in the streets, with the shells still whining overhead and with the riverside suburbs still being mopped up, people of this famous University city seem pleased to see us.

The fighting here has been the stiffest that this U.S. First Division has had since Aachen, much of it house-to-house, while there was really tough fighting for the barracks, yet the people are out in the streets willing to guide and help us.

I went straight to the town hall, where I was rather alarmed to find three German uniformed policemen at the door; however, they saluted smartly and I went in to try to find the mayor.

The staff was all present and one of the girl secretaries with a sense of humour gave me a "welcome to Bonn" booklet written in English.

She said she was sorry I could not see the mayor because the old-so-and-so had escaped across the Rhine last night. But would I care to see the chief of police?

Later I went out to see the university, guarded by one group of Germans after another, and they explained without bitterness how it had been destroyed by the RAF, though Beethoven's house still miraculously stands. It was hard to believe that all this morning we had been fighting tanks and self-propelled guns while even now German shells were whistling in.

By this time, about sixty German special constables had been rounded up for duty, and the Chief of Police was telling an American officer which ones he considered as "untrustworthy Nazis." A twin-engined German jet plane caused us some anxiety but did no harm.

We had come to Bonn through almost undamaged suburbs, while children played in the streets within a mile of the shooting, and this air of wild unreality had persisted throughout the day.

The Germans had been plastering the roads with depressed flak, like they did at Cologne, but here the roads were full of a fantastic mixture of the polyglot groups – Ukrainians, Yugoslavs, French and Belgians, in the main, with here and there an Italian, all making their way to the rear, without escort.

We stopped a group of buxom Russian women and I asked how things had been, and one of them said "Awful. For two years and nine months we have worked in their factories, and there were many police who thrashed and beat us, but now it is better." And all the old dames howled with laughter.

Prisoners are still coming in fast – many were taken in Bonn, and there are lorry loads of them again today.

I asked them where they were going, and they just said they did not know.

19 March 1945

BERLIN'S BIGGEST DAY RAID

BERLIN got its biggest day raid of the war yesterday.

More than 1,300 Liberators and Forts of the U.S. Eighth Air Force attacked communications in the city and armament plants in the industrial suburbs. They were escorted by 700 fighters.

The previous biggest day attack was on February 26, when 1,200 bombers took part.

The Schlesischer railway centre and the North Station freight yards, both within two miles of the centre of the capital were attacked by about 1,000 of the heavy bombers.

The remainder attacked the Rhein Metal Borsig plant at Tegel, six miles north-west of the centre, and a tank factory at Henningsdorf, five miles further out.

21 March 1945

ARCHBISHOP WANTS 'KILL AT SIGHT' JUSTICE ON HITLER AND NAZI BOSSES

THE Archbishop of York (Dr. Garbett) declared in the House of Lords last evening that the master criminals of the Nazi Reich should be decreed outlaws of humanity so that anyone who caught them would have the right to put them to death at once.

His speech came as the climax to demands that legal procedure should not be allowed to foil speedy justice on the enemies of civilisation, and that the "political status" of men like Hitler and Mussolini should not be allowed to obscure the fact that they are brutal criminals.

The answer of Lord Simon, for the Government, was that it was absolutely essential, for the future of the world, that international law should be strengthened.

Nothing would strengthen it more than the execution of speedy justice on war criminals. But it had to be realised that if guilty men were to be properly identified, it was inevitable that the number of cases brought to trial would fall far short of the wickedness that had been done.

▶ Field-Marshal Montgomery talks to the men of the Black Watch shortly before they start their assault over the River Rhine.

24 March 1945

ALLIES BURST ACROSS RHINE AGAIN

TANKS STRIKING 20 MILES FROM FRANKFURT

AT a time when the world is awaiting news of an all-out thrust into the Ruhr, Allied Supreme H.Q. announces this morning that the U.S. Third Army has burst across the Rhine, about 150 miles upstream from Montgomery's front.

Tanks and troops are pouring further into the Reich with an almost complete lack of opposition.

Berlin says the new crossing was made by American amphibious

tanks at Oppenheim, 12½ miles south of Mainz, and some 70 miles up the Rhine from the Remagen bridgehead, now 31 miles long and 10 miles deep.

The new bridgehead is firmly established about twenty miles from the city of Frankfurt-on-Main.

First crossings were made during Thursday night without air or artillery preparation.

According to Allied front line reports the first wave of troops paddled across the river in rubber boats at 10.25 p.m.

Caught completely by surprise, the Germans failed to fire a single round of artillery for two hours.

By dawn considerable infantry forces were on the east bank, and were pushing deeper into Germany.

Then a couple of Hun jet planes appeared over the beachhead and were promptly knocked down.

IKE WARNS RUHR WOMEN

A special warning from General Eisenhower to the women of the Ruhr was broadcast last night.

Many, he said, had heeded his previous warning to leave the Ruhr danger zones.

"But some of you," he said, "asked how the family can survive without wages or rations. WAGES AND RATIONS ARE OF NO USE TO THE DEAD.

"Women of the Ruhr! Thousands of you have acted already. Those of you who have not done so, act now. Out of the Ruhr! Out of the danger zone! Out of the war!"

▶ The Allies constructed bridges made of boats to take men, vehicles and supplies across the Rhine.

26 March 1945

MONTY SAID – "GOOD HUNTING"

"OVER the Rhine, then, let us go and good hunting to you all," said Field-Marshal Montgomery in an R-Day message to his troops.

He said:

"On the seventh of February I told you we were going into the ring for the final and last round.

"There would be no time limit. We would continue fighting until our opponent was knocked out.

"The last round is going very well on both sides of the ring – and overhead. It will be interesting to see how much longer the

Germans can stand it. The enemy, in fact, has been driven into a corner and he cannot escape.

"Twenty-one Army Group will now cross the Rhine.

"And having crossed the Rhine we will crack about in the plains of Northern Germany, chasing the enemy from pillar to post."

CHURCHILL SAID – "I REJOICE TO BE WITH YOU"

THE Prime Minister, in his message to 21st Army Group, said:

"I rejoice to be with the Chief of the Imperial General Staff at Field-Marshal Montgomery's headquarters of 21st Army Group during this memorable battle of forcing the Rhine.

"British soldiers – it will long be told how, with our Canadian brothers and valiant United States Allies, this superb task was accomplished.

"Once the river line is pierced and the crust of German resistance is broken, decisive victory in Europe will be near."

➡ Winston Churchill and Field-Marshal Montgomery cross the Rhine.

◗ Churchill steps ashore after crossing the Rhine with Allied forces.

DEMPSEY HAS IT PLANNED

From GEORGE McCARTHY,
on the Rhine, Sunday

CAPTAIN Miles Christopher Dempsey, of the Royal Berkshire Regiment, reached Cologne with the British Army of Occupation in December, 1918.

He is on the Rhine again today.

Now he is Lieutenant-General Sir Miles Dempsey, Commander of the British Second Army, and his troops, brilliantly led throughout a brilliant campaign, are crossing one of the broadest streams in Europe, the great water highway of which the Germans love to sing.

He is 48 years old and his fair hair is touched with grey. But he carries his slim, neat figure with the buoyancy of a youth.

For a month now, while Canadian and British troops under the command of General Crerar were winning the battle between the rivers, he has been planning the Rhine crossing.

He already knows what will follow and his provisional plans

are made. I talked with him half an hour before the battle began. We sat outside his caravan in the warm sunlight of this wonderful early spring.

He was confident that the battle would be won and won quickly and he believed that, when it was over, the German Army in the West would be almost at its end. We talked of the Commandos and I said that I knew the commanding officer of a certain Commando. "Oh, yes," he said, "you mean X," naming the very man.

I asked him if he knew all his battalion commanders. "I think I know most of them," he said. "You see they are the important men; if they are not right, nothing can be right."

He can speak there with experience, for when this war began he was in command of a battalion of the Berkshires. In France he had a brigade and later a division, and he arrived in the Near East as one of Monty's corps commanders. Dempsey is a shy man and a correct man. You cannot think of him wearing a Montgomery beret with a cluster of regimental badges. He never appears in corduroys, although he is tolerant of those of his staff who affect some new sartorial elegance.

He dislikes all publicity. "Don't write about me," he says, "write about the Second Army." He likes to live quietly and his caravans rest always some miles from his army headquarters.

Dempsey is a bachelor and a shy bachelor, but his friends say that he has all the social graces; that he dances as well as he hunts and he is a superb horseman.

He likes cricket, which he plays well – a left-hand bowler and a right-hand bat. He is naturally left handed and writes with his left hand.

One of his A.D.C.s is a minor authority on cricket and another, son of a famous horse trainer, can talk on level terms about horses.

His personal staff are his warmest admirers, which is itself a tribute to the man.

His friends, including Monty, call him Bimbo, but when I asked him how he earned that endearment he preferred to stay silent, although I fancied he blushed slightly.

NO POSTURES

But despite his nickname, Dempsey is not the man of whom others tell anecdotes. He is too naturally retiring, has no eccentricities, no postures, no sense of personal dramatics.

Yet he has a nice way. When the battle began it was the task of Bomber Command to wipe out the town of Wesel on the Rhine. Dempsey wanted to congratulate Bomber Harris on his achievement and went round his staff asking for the exact words of the old nursery rhyme, "Pop goes the weasel."

When he had all the words right, but not until he had them right, he decided to send Harris the message: "THAT'S THE WAY THE MONEY GOES," and left it to him to puzzle out the good news that Wesel had gone pop.

But don't imagine that the man who commands the Second Army is too genial or too gentle for his job. He believes that the thugs of the German Army, the paratroops and the S.S. men, must be exterminated. He hates war, but he hates brutality even more.

He is especially out to get the German General Heydrich, the commander of the paratroops. He fought him first in Sicily, he chased him halfway up Italy, and he even threw a Commando party into his H.Q. Heydrich escaped that time in pyjamas, but it may be that his fate is fast approaching.

HE'LL KEEP CALM

Whatever happens this week Dempsey will be calm. He will make his usual daily calls – it is typical of him that he always telephones his corps commanders to say what time they can see him – and he will return to his caravans and to Gertie.

Gertie is quite a feature of the camp. It is a goose captured by a Commando officer and presented to the Army Commander for his pot. But Dempsey grew fond of Gertie and Gertie of him. So the goose is there today basking in the sun. Only a few days ago was a major mistake discovered. Gertie was found to be, not a she but a he, and hopes of eggs have been abandoned.

Already Heydrich and all the lesser Heydrichs must be shivering in their jackboots; for this week-end Miles Dempsey, the Berkshire captain, has thrown his magnificent Second Army across the Rhine.

◗ The bodies of German soldiers lie on the Waal Bridge in Nijmegen.

THE NAVY HAS HOISTED WHITE ENSIGN ON THE SOIL OF GERMANY

with the Royal Navy in Germany

THE Navy has hoisted the White Ensign on German soil. It was run up on a roadside near the Rhine where Navy personnel waited for the cross-river assault.

The Navy was called in because the engines of the Army's usual craft are not strong enough for the Rhine current, which at this point – opposite the east bank town of Rees – is about four knots.

Naval officers, sailors and Marines are farther inland in Europe than they have ever been before. They brought their sea-landing craft from Antwerp to camps stretching south from Nijmegen, the Dutch town across the border from Germany.

The force was formed in Britain in February and brought to Germany through Antwerp in small units called "Molcabs" – "Mobile landing craft advanced bases."

A number of vessels, some for personnel and vehicles and the rest for supplies, were taken from Antwerp to Nijmegen partly by canal.

Others made the whole journey from Antwerp by road. Sailors sat in their craft as the boats were carried along the Dutch roads.

27 March 1945

HITLER'S RHINE DEFENCE ZONE HAS CRACKED

MONTY BREAKS OUT: PATTON 70 MILES INSIDE

GENERALS EISENHOWER, BRADLEY, PATTON AND HODGES YESTERDAY MET IN THE REMAGEN BRIDGEHEAD FOR WHAT WAS OFFICIALLY DESCRIBED AS A "SIGNIFICANT CONFERENCE."

THE Allied offensive over the Rhine is developing at sensational speed along the whole front.

One of Patton's tank spearheads, racing into Bavaria, was last night reported nearing the town of Wurzburg, which is seventy miles east of the Rhine. Another armoured column has entered the great city of Frankfurt-on-Main.

To the north, German resistance on the right-hand flank of Montgomery's salient appears to have cracked. British airborne troops have already gone over to the offensive and the U.S. Army is eighteen miles east of the Rhine.

A security black-out has been imposed on parts of this sector.

"NEXT FORTY-EIGHT HOURS . . ."

Allied forces in the bridgeheads between Montgomery and Patton are also driving forward. Indications are that the enemy's Rhine defence system has virtually collapsed.

Sertorius, Nazi commentator, admitted a "rapid deterioration" in the German position and said the next forty-eight hours would show whether Patton intends to thrust toward Czechoslovakia or wheel northward into the heart of the Reich.

KING THANKS IKE AND MONTY

Telegrams were sent by the King to General Eisenhower and Field-Marshal Montgomery yesterday congratulating them on "a military achievement of incalculable significance to the whole world."

To Monty the King said: "I send my warmest congratulations to you personally and to all in the 21st Army Group on the outstanding success of your recent operations.

"Your triumphant passage of the Rhine into the heart of the enemy territory has stirred us all very deeply, and I am more proud than I can say of the gallant part that my sailors, soldiers and airmen have played in it."

The message to Eisenhower expressed "gratitude to all those in all Services who have won this great and glorious victory."

THE MEN WHO DID IT!

THE victory of the Rhine makes history. The blow from the north, which must have struck a chill into the hearts of such Germans as still have the capacity to think and feel, was not unexpected. Its location was a fairly easy guess. But in what manner, precisely, the assault would be launched was known only to the Allied commanders whose work evokes the highest admiration. Let us, therefore, pay tribute to Eisenhower; to Montgomery; and to the brilliant team of generals who have conducted the actual fighting. The result of their work has given the nation the greatest thrill since D-Day.

All their splendid troops share in the victory which, symbolic as well as actual – for the Rhine is the immemorial bastion of the Reich – means that the "last round" has indeed begun and that Germany, already out on her feet, will soon be taking the count.

For once, the names of the British units taking part have not been withheld. They have already been published, but we celebrate the occasion by repeating them.

15th SCOTTISH; 51st HIGHLAND; 79th ARMOURED;
1st COMMANDO BRIGADE; 6th AIRBORNE DIVISION.

Regiments named are:
THE BLACK WATCH.
ARGYLL AND SUTHERLAND HIGHLANDERS.
ROYAL BERKSHIRES.
THE ROYALS.
CHESHIRE REGIMENT.
81st FIELD ARTILLERY.
CANADIAN HIGHLAND LIGHT INFANTRY.
MANCHESTER REGIMENT.
ROYAL SCOTS FUSILIERS.
ROYAL SCOTS.
KING'S OWN SCOTTISH BORDERERS.
ROYAL TANK REGIMENT.
GORDON HIGHLANDERS.
MIDDLESEX REGIMENT.
CAMERONIANS.
102nd ANTI-TANK REGIMENT
(NORTHUMBERLAND HUSSARS).
E. RIDING OF YORKSHIRE YEOMANRY.
WESTMINSTER DRAGOONS.
DUKE OF CORNWALL'S LIGHT INFANTRY.
WORCESTERSHIRE REGIMENT.

HAMPSHIRE REGIMENT.
DORSETSHIRE REGIMENT.
SOMERSET LIGHT INFANTRY.
WILTSHIRE REGIMENT.
NORTHAMPTONSHIRE YEOMANRY

A mighty list! To it has to be added, most importantly, the R.A.F. And the Navy! Well, the Navy was there, too – one hundred miles from salt water. A great day for British arms. Every man and woman in these islands, every person with near and dear ones at the Front, will feel glad and proud of the Old Country and the men it breeds.

◆ Two teenage German prisoners, both with less than 12 weeks' training, are captured with more than 8,000 others as Montgomery's troops crossed the Rhine.

FOUR-YEAR MEN WERE GIVEN ONLY 7 DAYS' LEAVE

ALTHOUGH soldiers who have served four years overseas are entitled to twenty-eight days' home leave Private Harry McQuillan and Private Jim Wood, both of Stoke-on-Trent, came back from the Middle East and were given just seven days' leave each to spend with their families.

Both had been abroad for more than four years, and they are now "somewhere in Europe" just a fortnight after they returned to this country.

At McQuillan's home yesterday, his wife told the *Daily Mirror*: "The two children and I were sure we'd have him home for four weeks, but he was not smiling when he came to the door. He said right away, 'I've only got a week.'

"A week – after nearly five years away from us," she declared. "And then we had little more than two days of it together.

"Harry was all over the place, trying to get the extension due to him . . . But his efforts came to nothing and he had to go back."

Private Wood's young wife was so distressed that she has not left the house since he went back.

Both families have protested to War Minister Sir James Grigg and reported the facts to their M.P., Mr. Ellis Smith.

28 March **1945**

IKE SAYS "IT'S A WHIPPED ARMY, BUT DARN TOUGH FIGHTING YET"

GENERAL EISENHOWER said yesterday that the main German defence line had been broken in the crossing of the Rhine.

The Germans, he said, according to Reuter, have no strength to make any future stand such as they have already made.

But he added this warning:

"I would not have you think I have written off this war.

"No one knows what the Germans can do within their own country. They are trying to do everything they can. I believe so far as they are able, the Germans will stand and fight wherever we find them.

"I would say that the Germans as a military force on the Western Front, are a whipped army. That does not mean the front cannot be formed somewhere where our maintenance is stretched to the limit and their defensive means can better be brought to bear.

"There will be some darn tough fighting before it's over."

5 April **1945**

MONTGOMERY THREATENS BREMEN

280,000 NAZI PRISONERS IN FORTNIGHT

TWO HUNDRED AND EIGHTY THOUSAND prisoners have been captured by the Allies on the Western Front in the 14

days ended last night, not counting wounded who have fallen into our hands. It is the most sensational achievement in modern military history.

The figure, more clearly than any details of advances, indicates how crippling has been the blow suffered by the German armies.

A comparison is the 286,000 prisoners captured by the Russians in the SIX WEEKS which culminated in the German defeat at Stalingrad. In two weeks it almost equals the total of 291,000 prisoners for the whole Tunisia campaign, from mid-March to early May, 1943.

And in addition to the Allied haul, even according to conservative estimates there are another 50,000 Germans encircled in the Ruhr.

7 April **1945**

RUSSIANS NEAR BERLIN ARE ON MOVE AGAIN:

VIENNA NOW HALF-ENCIRCLED

RUSSIAN troops are making good progress towards Berlin against bitter resistance, according to reliable reports in Moscow.

These reports cannot be officially confirmed because there is a strict security silence on the campaign west of the Oder.

Rapid progress is being made on the Vienna front. The city is apparently already half-surrounded.

16 April **1945**

NO VE-DAY UNTIL EAST FRONT GOES

By BILL GREIG

EXPECTATIONS OF VE-DAY BEING ANNOUNCED WITHIN A FEW DAYS ARE PREMATURE

The Cabinet have decided most definitely that there can be no VE-Day here until the German Army facing the Russians has also been broken up.

This may happen at any moment, but there will be no celebrations here while something like 120 German divisions still maintain an almost intact line facing the Red Army in Germany.

"TREACHERY" WARNING BY HITLER

HITLER'S Order of the Day to his East Front forces said:

"For the last time the Jewish Bolshevist arch enemy has hurled his masses into an attack.

"He is trying to pulverise Germany and terminate our people. You soldiers on the Eastern Front know well from your own experience the fate which is in store for all German women, maidens and children.

"The old men and the children will be murdered. Women and maidens will be debased to the level of barrack-room harlots. The rest will be packed off to Siberia."

"ALL PREPARED"

"We have foreseen this blow. Since last January everything has been done to build a strong front line. The enemy is being met with formidable artillery and infantry.

"The front has been strengthened by shock units, reserves and Volkssturm.

"This time Bolshevism will suffer the fate which has always befallen Asia. It must and will bleed to death in front of the capital.

"He who in this hour does not do his duty is a traitor to our people. The regiment or the division which abandons its position behaves basely, execrably."

"I WARN YOU"

"I warn you to keep an eye on the few treacherous officers and soldiers who to save their miserable skins are in Russian pay, and perhaps German uniform, and will fight against us.

"He who gives the order to retreat – unless he is very well known to you – is to be arrested at once and if necessary to be shot on the spot, regardless of rank.

"If in the days and weeks to come, every soldier does his duty, then the last onslaught from Asia will collapse as in the end the break-through of our enemies in the West will collapse.

"Berlin remains German. Vienna will become German again. Europe will never be Russian."

"EMPTY WORD"

"Unite and pledge yourselves with one voice to defend, not the empty conception of the Fatherland, but your own country, your women, your children.

"At this hour the whole of the German people looks towards you, my soldiers, in the East, hoping that by your steadfastness, your fanaticism, your weapons, Bolshevism will drown in a sea of blood.

"The moment fate has disposed of this most formidable war criminal of all times, the turning point of this war will come."

NO VE-DAY TILL ALL REICH IS OCCUPIED

General Eisenhower yesterday told correspondents at a SHAEF command post that "There will be no VE-Day until Germany is completely occupied, including all pockets of resistance, and the German Army completely destroyed."

Bill Greig writes:

THE War Cabinet will be in almost continuous session from today onwards.

Ministers have received instructions to remain within easy reach of Downing-street in view of the possibility that decisions of vital importance may have to be taken at short notice.

One point will arise from the linking up of the British and Russian armies.

If fighting is still in progress then, a much closer co-ordination of tactics will be required.

A joint command may be necessary in certain areas.

There will also be problems as to occupation and the setting up of military tribunals in areas jointly occupied.

When the fighting ceases, it is possible that both British and American troops will be in the Russian zone of Germany and arrangements for their withdrawal will have to be made.

FREED BRITISH AND AMERICANS ARE TO BE FLOWN TO ENGLAND

From GEORGE McCARTHY, Fallingbostel (Germany), Tuesday

IT is hoped that every man freed yesterday in Stalags 357 and 118 will be flown straight to England.

Today and tomorrow the 500 British and American sick will be evacuated from the stalags to nearby British hospitals.

When they have been brought out, a start will be made on the healthy.

All British and Americans will be taken first to a nearby marshalling area, medically inspected, given good meals and rested.

They will then go to the nearest transport airport and be flown home.

Once the organisation begins to operate, it is believed that it will be possible to move 500 men a day.

But already the men know the joys of freedom. Last night they got supplies of food and cigarettes, and today when I visited the camp the first lorry load of white bread came in.

Men snatched the loaves from the lorries and, running with them into the huts, cried out to their comrades: "Look, white bread, real white bread."

GUNS MOVE UP ON BERLIN

SOUND of the artillery barrage from the fronts near Berlin is hourly becoming louder in the streets of the capital.

The German Overseas News Agency said this last night as Red Army tanks were driving across the last eighteen miles before the city boundary. Swedish reports say there are half a million German troops massed in the capital for a last stand.

The Germans say that Zhukov's armies are converging on the capital round a sixty-mile arc from east of Eberswalde through the Seelow area to Furstenberg on the Oder, sixteen miles south of Frankfurt.

21 April 1945

EISENHOWER SAYS 'ENEMY IN THE WEST IS TOTTERING TO DEFEAT'

RUSSIANS FIGHT AROUND THE EDGE OF BERLIN

AS two Russian spearheads fought last night less than eight miles from the outskirts of Berlin, General Eisenhower declared in an Order of the Day that Hitler's armies in the west are "tottering on the threshold of defeat." An Allied Supreme Headquarters announcement said we would link up with the Russians in a few days.

Admitting that a Soviet spearhead is only eight miles from the boundary of Berlin, the German military spokesman revealed that another spearhead has penetrated even nearer.

Symbol of the Hun defeat, the Stars and Stripes, was raised last night – Hitler's birthday – over the ruins of the Nazi "holy city" of Nuremberg, where 3,000 S.S. troops became our prisoners.

23 April 1945

CIVILIANS STAMPEDE AS GUNS RAKE HUN CAPITAL

MEN, women and children streamed through the north-west suburbs of Berlin last night with only one thought in their minds – to get as far away from Berlin as possible.

Rumour spread that Goebbels himself had left Berlin, according to a British United Press message from Sweden.

Shells fell continuously and hit such well-known places as the Unter den Linden, the Brandenburg Gate and the Leipzigerstrasse.

The first uncensored stories of the war came out of Berlin on Saturday night.

Swedish newspapermen tried in vain to find the censors, so they phoned Stockholm and got their stories through right away. Later the line went dead.

The Stockholm *Dagens Nyheter* got this message:

"The fall of Berlin is expected to be a matter of a few days, possibly hours.

"Hundreds of thousands of Berliners are massing outside the shelters awaiting the official alert allowing them to enter.

"Hysterical men and women squeezed wounded soldiers out of underground trains."

➡ Troops from the U.S. First Army cross a broken bridge over the Elbe to greet Russian soldiers as the two armies link up at Torgau on 25 April.

LAST NIGHT GERMANY HAD NOT SURRENDERED: NEW HIMMLER OFFER LIKELY IN 48 HOURS

ALLIES READY FOR LAST MOVES – BUT FIGHT ON

GERMANY had not laid down her arms last night – whatever may happen in the next few days. Allied armies were still fighting on against German resistance. From the welter of rumours three points can be confirmed:

1. – Himmler did make an offer, through the Swede, Count Bernadotte, to surrender to Britain and the U.S. This was refused.
2. – As Himmler is head of the German Home Forces and therefore representative of the General Staff, we are prepared to accept surrender from him, in his military capacity, the moment it includes surrender to Russia as well.
3 .– There is absolutely no foundation for reports that this surrender has been offered or that a time limit has been set.

The next move lies with Himmler. In London last night it was confidently expected that he will approach the Allies again within the next forty-eight hours.

Before that there may be big news, and if that news includes the death of Hitler there will be no surprise.

The report that Hitler is suffering from cerebral haemorrhage is accepted with reserve. There is however good reason to believe that his days are numbered.

RED FLAG ON REICHSTAG

The Red Flag was hoisted over the German Reichstag yesterday.

And with the central Post Office also occupied, the Red Army hurled fresh forces into an all-out bid to crush the last core of resistance in the Reich capital, hoping to announce its fall on May Day (today).

Hamburg was meanwhile broadcasting a programme entitled "What Was Berlin?"

"Now," it said, "there are only memories."

➤ Two soldiers of the Russian Red Army in the ruins of Adolf Hitler's room in the Berlin Chancellery, one sprawling in Hitler's chair with his feet on the upturned table.

"GERMANY WILL BATTLE ON" HITLER DEAD

KILLED IN BERLIN, SAYS NEW FUEHRER, ADMIRAL DOENITZ

HITLER was killed in action yesterday afternoon, according to a

May 2, 1945

Page 7

Daily Mirror

Wednesday, May 2, 1945
No. 12,906   ONE PENNY
Registered at G.P.O. as a Newspaper.

"GERMANY WILL BATTLE ON"

HITLER DEAD

Killed in Berlin, says new Fuehrer, Admiral Doenitz

Adolf Hitler, leader of the Nazi Reich since January 30, 1933, the world's chief criminal, now dead at the age of fifty-six.

HITLER was killed in action yesterday afternoon, according to a broadcast from Hamburg at 10.30 last night.

His successor is Rear-Admiral Doenitz, the C.-in-C. of the German Navy, who made the announcement himself.

Doenitz said: "The Fuehrer has fallen at his command post in Berlin. He fell for Germany."

This is Doenitz

Admiral Doenitz, who directed the U-boat war, and who now styles himself Head of the Nazi Reich

"MY FIRST TASK," SAID DOE-NITZ, "IS TO SAVE THE GERMAN PEOPLE FROM DES-TRUCTION BY BOL-SHEVISM. IF ONLY FOR THIS TASK THE STRUGGLE WILL CONTINUE.

"Give me your confidence. Do your duty. Keep order. Only in this way shall we be able to prevent collapse.

The German announcement came just as the House of Commons rose.

After a roll of drums, Hamburg radio said :

"It is reported from the Fuehrer's headquarters that our Fuehrer, Adolf Hitler, has fallen this afternoon at his command post in the Reich Chancellery fighting to the last breath against Bolshevism and for Germany.

"On April 30 the Fuehrer appointed Grand Admiral Doenitz as his successor.

"Our new Fuehrer will speak to the German people."

The last reference to Hitler was in yesterday's

'Lay down your arms' —Graziani to his Army

MARSHAL GRAZIANI, commander of the Ligurian Army, who was captured by the Allies in Italy, said this over Rome radio last night:

"To Italian and German troops in Liguria, lay down your arms. For several days the German Supreme Command in Italy has not issued any orders and its whereabout are unknown. Under the circumstances, I took over the personal responsibility of signing unconditional surrender to the U.S. Command on April 29.

"Further resistance would not only be useless, but also dangerous for myself."

'Wait' is Churchill's tip to the Commons

MR. CHURCHILL told the Commons yesterday that he had no special statement to make about the war situation in Europe, but if information reached the Government this week—"as it might do"—he would tell the House.

It was not his idea that information should be kept back "until the exact occupation of all the particular zones."

Snowfire Girls: MARGARET

Margaret is essentially a man's girl. She likes the drinks that men like ; she appreciates good cooking and the finer points of most sports. And, as she is never separated from her Snowfire Beauty Makers, she is always good to look at.

Snowfire

BEAUTY MAKERS

For ever and a Date!

CREAM · POWDER · LIPSTICK

DANES ARE TAKING OVER FROM THE GERMAN ARMY

THE Danes are taking control in their own country again. Danish police in full uniform are again patrolling the streets of several towns, from which the Germans have withdrawn without incident.

This sensational news was reported by British United Press from Copenhagen, capital of Denmark, last night.

The Danish and German authorities, it was stated, are negotiating an agreement for the reinstatement of the Danish police all over the country.

Count Folke Bernadotte was yesterday reported to

have flown from Denmark with a German - Swedish agreement for the surrender of Nazi troops in both Denmark and Norway.

Danish underground sources reported that the movement of German troops from North to South Denmark had already begun.

Other sources believed that the Swedes had proposed—or the Huns had asked—that the German Army in Norway should go to Sweden to be disarmed there.

The Nazis want to get their troops into Sweden before

Continued on Back Page

CIVIL SERVANTS ARE ASKING FOR HIGHER PAY

WAGE increases and reduced hours are urged in resolutions tabled for the two-day Annual Conference of the Society of Civil Servants next week in London.

A general stepping-up of annual increments is sought in one resolution from the Midlands, which also urges a five-day working week for the Civil Service when hostilities cease.

Continued on Back Page

Where now? *Hitler was presumed to have died in his Chancellery on April 30. But what was certain was that his shadow would continue to stalk the world for years to come.*

(May, 1945)

broadcast from Hamburg at 10.30 last night.

His successor is Rear-Admiral Doenitz, the C.-in-C. of the German Navy, who made the announcement himself.

Doenitz said: "The Fuehrer has fallen at his command post in Berlin. He fell for Germany."

"MY FIRST TASK," SAID DOENITZ, "IS TO SAVE THE GERMAN PEOPLE FROM DESTRUCTION BY BOLSHEVISM, IF ONLY FOR THIS TASK THE STRUGGLE WILL CONTINUE.

"Give me your confidence. Do your duty. Keep order. Only in this way shall we be able to prevent collapse."

The German announcement came just as the House of Commons rose.

After a roll of drums, Hamburg radio said:

"It is reported from the Fuehrer's headquarters that our Fuehrer, Adolf Hitler, has fallen this afternoon at his command post in the Reich Chancellery fighting to the last breath against Bolshevism and for Germany.

"On April 30 the Fuehrer appointed Grand Admiral Doenitz as his successor.

"Our new Fuehrer will speak to the German people."

◗ The city of Hamburg lies in ruins and apparently deserted on the day of Germany's surrender, 3 May 1945.

1,000,000 NAZIS SURRENDER – AND DOENITZ LOSES HIS SOUTH REDOUBT

THE HUNS HAVE SIGNED AWAY THEIR SOUTHERN REDOUBT. FIELD MARSHAL SIR HAROLD ALEXANDER'S FORCES CAN NOW ADVANCE UNHINDERED FROM ITALY TO WITHIN THREE MILES OF BERCHTESGADEN, ONCE HITLER'S ALPINE HANG-OUT.

This, the first unconditional surrender by German armies in Europe in this war, came into effect at 2 p.m. (Double Summer Time) yesterday. It embraces up to 1,000,000 men in Italy and Western Austria.

Now Germany's new Fuehrer, Grand Admiral Doenitz has 30,000 square miles less land under his sway.

And his northern redoubt is shrinking under the advances of Field-Marshal Montgomery and the Red Army. Yesterday the British 11th Armoured Division captured the Baltic port of Lubeck, and the Red Army seized Rostock.

BERLIN SURRENDERS: 70,000 SEIZED

GARRISON of Berlin, headed by General Webling, laid down their arms and surrendered to the Red Army yesterday afternoon.

This was announced by Marshal Stalin at ten o'clock last night.

Up to 9 p.m. the Russians had captured more than 70,000 Germans in the capital.

Stalin credits this great victory to troops of both Marshals Zhukov and Koniev, who – "After stubborn street battles completed the rout of the Berlin garrison and captured the city of Berlin, the capital of Germany, the centre of German Imperialism and the heart of German aggression."

Last night Moscow fired twenty-four salvos of 324 guns.

HITLER'S GOOD DEED

HITLER is officially dead. He has passed from the scene of his infamies and will not appear again.

It would be easy to enumerate his crimes; to compose an epitaph of denunciation. We shall do no such thing. On the contrary we wish to emphasise one aspect of his baleful career which stands forth as a positive good.

Hitler demonstrated to all men the depth to which a nation can fall. More important than that he disclosed to the world the real intentions of German policy and the true character of the German people. In this revelation mankind received a priceless gift, if mankind has the wit to use it rightly.

POWER LUST

Hitler was a symbol of the German lust for power. That is the explanation of the man. Bismarck unified the Germans and drove to the East. The Kaiser developed naval power to lay the foundation, as he thought, of world domination. Hitler was the inheritor of both these traditions. His special opportunity was that he was able to "cash in" on the evils of poverty and mass unemployment. German policy has been consistent and cumulative. The character of the people has not changed. It combines submissiveness to authority with arrogance, ambition, and complete indifference to the sufferings of others. It has been ideal soil for the growth of tyranny.

No normal person could have imagined that when Hitler's turn came to direct German policy he would carry it out with such satanic brutality. But now we know. In him we see the flowering of German mentality. We should be thankful for the lesson.

WHAT MIGHT HAVE BEEN

Make no mistake. If Hitler had waited a few more years he would have found this country even less prepared than it was in 1939. His power would have been unassailable. Our Government would have been murdered in its sleep.

Never must the slothful years return. Who shall say that there are not in the world other Hitlers waiting to rise up if the time comes ripe? The end of German power is the end, or ought to be, of that evil thing the "balance of power". We can make it the beginning of a collective system, thus to fashion a world in which no man anywhere can have the chance to debase the human race.

Out of evil cometh good. It may be – and if we have the wisdom and determination it will be – that the nightmare of Nazidom is but the ugly prelude to a dream of peace and good will destined to come true.

◀ A female Russian Army soldier on traffic duty and a British soldier in Berlin.

▶ Two Russian soldiers talk to their American counterparts in Berlin.

The figures for the great new surrender include 250,000 naval personnel – the surrender embraced all naval ships in the areas.

IT IS TRIUMPH DAY FOR FIELD-MARSHAL MONTGOMERY AND HIS MEN. THEY HAVE BEATEN THE HUN TO HIS KNEES ALONG THE WHOLE OF THEIR FRONT, AND HAVE WRITTEN "FINIS" TO THE GERMAN REICH.

And today they bring salvation to the starving millions of Holland, and freedom to the people of Denmark, crushed for five long years under the Nazi jackboot. Amsterdam, Rotterdam, The Hague and the other cities of Holland will all be free today.

The Canadian Army, which takes over Holland, has had plans ready for over a week to rush food supplies in.

Only two major centres of German resistance now remain – in Norway and the shattered redoubt in Austria and Czechoslovakia.

In addition, the Germans still hold pockets on the west coast of France, the Channel Islands, Dunkirk, some Polish coastal territory, strips of East Prussia and Latvia, and a few pockets in the south.

8 May 1945

VE-DAY!

IT'S OVER IN THE WEST

TODAY is VE-Day – the day for which the British people have fought and endured five years, eight months and four days of war.

With unconditional surrender accepted by Germany's last remaining leaders, the war in Europe is over except for the actions of fanatical Nazis in isolated pockets, such as Prague. The Prime Minister will make an official announcement – in accordance with arrangements between Britain, Russia and the U.S. – at 3 o'clock this afternoon.

ALL TODAY AND TOMORROW ARE PUBLIC HOLIDAYS IN BRITAIN, IN CELEBRATION OF OUR VICTORY.

We also remember and salute with gratitude and pride the men and women who suffered and died to make triumph possible – and the men still battling in the East against another cruel enemy who is still in the field.

LONDON HAD JOY NIGHT

DAILY MIRROR REPORTER

PICCADILLY CIRCUS, VE-EVE

THIS is IT – and we are all going nuts! There are thousands of us in Piccadilly Circus. The police say more than 10,000 – and that's a conservative estimate.

5 May 1945

ALL HUN FORCES IN NORTH-WEST GERMANY, HOLLAND AND DENMARK GIVE IN

TRIUMPH DAY FOR MONTY'S MEN

ANOTHER MILLION IN BAG: BIGGEST MASS SURRENDER OF WAR

AT 8 a.m. today more than 1,000,000 Germans in Holland, Denmark and North-West Germany are laying down their arms to Field-Marshal Montgomery in the biggest mass surrender of German forces since the Armistice of 1918.

The bag of prisoners in Italy is estimated at 900,000, so that in three days about 2,000,000 Germans have gone out of the war.

Daily Mirror ⒉ MAY 8

Tuesday, May 8, 1945
No. 12,911 — ONE PENNY
Registered at G.P.O. as a Newspaper.

VE-DAY!

IT'S OVER IN THE WEST

TODAY is VE-Day—the day for which the British people have fought and endured five years, eight months and four days of war.

With unconditional surrender accepted by Germany's last remaining leaders, the war in Europe is over except for the actions of fanatical Nazis in isolated pockets, such as Prague.

The Prime Minister will make an official announcement—in accordance with arrangements between Britain, Russia and the U.S.—at 3 o'clock this afternoon.

ALL TODAY AND TO-MORROW ARE PUBLIC HOLIDAYS IN BRITAIN, IN CELEBRATION OF OUR VICTORY.

We also remember and salute with gratitude and pride the men and women who suffered and died to make triumph possible—and the men still battling in the East against another cruel enemy who is still in the field.

War winners broadcast today

You will hear the voices of the King, Field-Marshals Montgomery and Alexander, and General Eisenhower when they broadcast over the B.B.C. Home Service tonight.

After the King's speech, at 9 p.m., and separated from it by the news bulletin, comes "Victory Report," a special programme which will contain the recorded voices of Ike and Monty, and other famous personalities of the war.

Additional features of the B.B.C. Home programme, which will end at 2 a.m. to-morrow, include, at 8 p.m., an address by the Archbishop of Canterbury at a Thanksgiving Service for Victory, and at 8.30 a tribute to the King.

★ VE-SCENE TRAFALGAR SQUARE

It was a high old time in Trafalgar-square last night. Everybody wanted to climb something. This party of Wrens and Allied soldiers celebrated by clambering on to the lions. Army policemen present—like Nelson on his column—turned a blind eye.

London had joy night

"Daily Mirror" Reporter

PICCADILLY CIRCUS, VE-EVE.

THIS is IT—and we are all going nuts! There are thousands of us in Piccadilly-circus. The police say more than 10,000—and that's a conservative estimate.

We are dancing the Conga and the jig and "Knees up, Mother Brown," and we are singing and whistling, and blowing paper trumpets.

The idea is to make a noise. We are. Even above the roar of the motors of low-flying bombers "shooting up" the city.

We are dancing around Eros in the black-out, but there is a glow from a bonfire up Shaftesbury-avenue and a news reel cinema has lit its canopy lights for the first time in getting on for six years.

A huge V sign glares down over Leicester Square. And gangs of girls and soldiers of all the Allied nations are waving rattles and shouting and climbing lamp-posts and swarming over cars that have become bogged down in this struggling, swirling mass of celebrating Londoners.

We have been waiting from two o'clock to celebrate. We went home at six when it seemed that the news of VE-Day would never come, but we are back now.

And on a glorious night we are making the most of it. A paper-hatted throng is trying to pull me out of this telephone box now. I hold the door tight, but the din from Piccadilly Circus is drowning my voice.

It is past midnight. We are still singing. A group of men liberated from German prison camps are yelling—"Roll out the Barrel."

"We sang it when we went to France in 1939 and we sang it as we tried to get out in 1940," they told me. "Now we sing it for victory."

Amid terrific cheers a New Zealand sailor climbed on the bonnet of a bus and from there to the roof.

He stood there swaying above the crowds as the American army swarmed up

◆ Continued on Back Page

Vast crowds cheer Prime Minister Winston Churchill after his victory speech from a balcony in Whitehall.

We are dancing the Conga and the jig and 'Knees up, Mother Brown', and we are singing and whistling, and blowing paper trumpets.

The idea is to make a noise. We are. Even above the roar of the motors of low-flying bombers "shooting up" the city.

We are dancing around Eros in the black-out, but there is a glow from a bonfire up Shaftesbury Avenue and a news reel cinema has lit its canopy lights for the first time in getting on for six years.

A huge V sign glares down over Leicester Square. And gangs of girls and soldiers of all the Allied nations are waving rattles and shouting and climbing lamp-posts and swarming over cars that have become bogged down in this struggling, swirling mass of celebrating Londoners.

We have been waiting from two o'clock to celebrate. We went home at six when it seemed that the news of VE-Day would never come, but we are back now.

And on a glorious night we are making the most of it. A paper-hatted throng is trying to pull me out of this telephone box now. I hold the door tight, but the din from Piccadilly Circus is drowning my voice.

It is past midnight. We are still singing. A group of men liberated from German prison camps are yelling – "Roll out the Barrel."

"We sang it when we went to France in 1939 and we sang it as we tried to get out in 1940," they told me. "Now we sing it for victory."

◀ Residents of Denmark Street, London, celebrate by hanging out the washing as mentioned in the popular song of the time "We're going to hang out the washing on the Siegfried Line".

◀ Field-Marshal Montgomery offers his thanks to his troops and his hopes for peace.

9 May 1945

MINUTE PAST MIDNIGHT

THE final total surrender documents were signed by the Germans and the three Allies yesterday IN BERLIN.

The Channel Isles were to be freed at once.

Hostilities in Europe ended officially at 12.01 a.m. today.

---

21 ARMY GROUP

PERSONAL MESSAGE FROM THE C-IN-C

(To be read out to all Troops)

1. On this day of victory in Europe I feel I would like to speak to all who have served and fought with me during the last few years. What I have to say is very simple, and quite short.

2. I would ask you all to remember those of our comrades who fell in the struggle. They gave their lives that others might have freedom, and no man can do more than that. I believe that He would say to each one of them:

    "Well done, thou good and faithful servant."

3. And we who remain have seen the thing through to the end; we all have a feeling of great joy and thankfulness that we have been preserved to see this day.

    We must remember to give the praise and thankfulness where it is due:

    "This is the Lord's doing, and it is marvellous in our eyes."

4. In the early days of this war the British Empire stood alone against the combined might of the axis powers. And during those days we suffered some great disasters; but we stood firm: on the defensive, but striking blows where we could. Later we were joined by Russia and America; and from then onwards the end was in no doubt. Let us never forget what we owe to our Russian and American allies; this great allied team has achieved much in war; may it achieve even more in peace.

5. Without doubt, great problems lie ahead; the world will not recover quickly from the upheaval that has taken place; there is much work for each one of us.

    I would say that we must face up to that work with the same fortitude that we faced up to the worst days of this war. It may be that some difficult times lie ahead for our country, and for each one of us personally. If it happens thus, then our discipline will pull us through; but we must remember that the best discipline implies the subordination of self for the benefit of the community.

6. It has been a privilege and an honour to command this great British Empire team in western Europe. Few commanders can have had such loyal service as you have given me. I thank each one of you from the bottom of my heart.

7. And so let us embark on what lies ahead full of joy and optimism. We have won the German war. Let us now win the peace.

8. Good luck to you all, wherever you may be.

B. L. Montgomery

Germany,
May, 1945.

Field-Marshal,
C.-in-C.,
21 Army Group.

Daily Mirror

MAY 9

Wednesday, May 9, 1945
No. 12,912   ONE PENNY
Registered at G.P.O. as a Newspaper.

♦ ♦ ♦

BRITAIN'S DAY OF REJOICING

This picture of VE-Day crowds jam-packing Whitehall is just one scene from thousands of similar scenes that marked the nation's great day of rejoicing. We reproduce a selection from them on pages 4, 5 and 8.

All day long the happy crowds paraded. They cheered, they waved flags, they flocked from place to place, determined not to miss a single sight on this day of days. The victory spirit was in everybody's blood.

Minute past midnight

THE final total surrender documents were signed by the Germans and the three Allies yesterday IN BERLIN. The Channel Isles were to be freed at once.

Hostilities in Europe ended officially at 12.1 a.m. today.

Churchill on page 3. King's speech last night on page 4.